# SANTHAL WORLDVIEW

## About the Editor

**Dr. Nita Mathur** is an anthropologist presently associated with the Indira Gandhi National Centre for the Arts where she coordinates collaborative programmes based on lifestyle studies. She is currently exploring the concepts of body, womb and seed through Santhal vocabulary. Apart from contributing a number of research articles in reputed journals and books, she is the author of *Cultural Rhythms in Emotions, Narratives and Dance* (in press).

# SANTHAL WORLDVIEW

*Edited by*

**NITA MATHUR**

INDIRA GANDHI NATIONAL CENTRE FOR THE ARTS
NEW DELHI

CONCEPT PUBLISHING COMPANY, NEW DELHI-110 059

The views expressed in this volume are those of the authors, and are not necessarily those of the editors or the publishers.

ISBN-81-7022-866-2

First Published 2001



*Published and Printed by*
Ashok Kumar Mittal
**Concept Publishing Company**
A/15-16, Commercial Block, Mohan Garden
NEW DELHI-110059 (India)

*Phones* : 5648039, 5649024
*Fax* : 091(11)5648053
*E-mail* : publishing@conceptpub.com

# CONTENTS

# INTRODUCTION

The Indira Gandhi National Centre for the Arts (IGNCA) is envisioned as a major resource centre engaged in redefining the arts in the larger matrix of culture and lifestyle of people. The Centre is engaged in evolving a multilayered, multidimensional model of lifestyle studies with emphasis on 'folk' tradition or *loka parampara*. The specific community studies take cognizance of the interrelatedness of nature, ecology, beliefs and practices, knowledge system and art works in an integrated framework. Research into various aspects of cultural communities as the Changpas of Ladakh, Gujars of Central Himalayas, Meiteis of Manipur, and Angamis of Nagaland, in the North; Visvakarmas and forest dwellers of Karnataka, and Mukkuvars of Tamil Nadu in the South; Santhals of West Bengal, Bihar and Orissa, and Bhuiyans of Orissa in the East; and Warlis of Maharashtra in the West have been undertaken.

The *loka parampara* studies accept that there is continuity between the intellectual, textual tradition (*sastra*) and its interpretation and application in lived life (*prayoga*). This is more than corroborated by the in-house projects on the Gaddis of Himachal Pradesh, millet or *bajara* growing communities of Rajasthan, and the Garhwal Himalaya communities given to performing Pandava dance theatre. Each of these exemplify the multiplicity of textual interpretations within a culture and across cultural groups. The interrelatedness of textual with oral tradition calls for exploration of some fundamental concepts which reflect people's understanding of the cosmos and the entire creation. This becomes particularly relevant in the case of cohesive communities — those that have been referred to as 'tribals' representing primordial, pristine vision and creativity.

For the purpose of comprehending a specific culture from a holistic perspective, the Santhal — a cohesive community in the eastern zone has been taken up for an in-depth study. This cultural group has been researched and written about extensively since the 19th century. There is, therefore, a vast storehouse of information from primary and secondary sources. The IGNCA has endeavoured to reconstruct different aspects of Santhal culture through an in-house project based on Santhal terms on body, womb and seed and a series of collaborative projects on the place of animals in society; sound, language and script; food and the scheme of cooking; healing practices and beliefs about after - life reflected in a distinctive painting tradition. Apart from the literary documentation, the Centre has generated audio and video tapes of Santhal music and the annual ritual of *pata puja* and acquired musical instruments of Santhals as part of its ethnographic collection. These are corroborated by an ambitious programme of developing soundscape of Santhals.

A seminar on Santhal Worldview, of which this publication is an outcome, was held in September 1997. It provided a meeting ground of researchers associated with the IGNCA's pursuit of comprehending the Santhal lifestyle on the one hand and representatives of the Santhal community on the other. This coming together of those with intellectual acumen and those with experience of being a part of Santhal culture called for **developing** an integrated, holistic database, **sharing** the experience, perspective, methods and models of analyses, and **fostering** dialogue between intellectual tradition of academics and wisdom tradition of Santhals themselves. The essays collected here address the fundamental themes of, (i) Nature and Culture; (ii) Sound and Language; and (iii) Lifestyle and Worldview. Evidently, Santhal worldview woven around indigenous understanding of human faculties of sustenance, experience and expression is replete with people's own interpretation of the nature of primal elements, cosmic order and consciousness.

**Nature and Culture :** The one idea which gets repeated in traditional thought and culture is the inseparability of nature and culture. There is an implicit acceptance of the fact that human beings constitute an integral part of nature. Lifestyles reaffirm the relationship between the various elements of nature and celebrate its rhythm in patterns of language, rituals, beliefs and different dimensions of culture. This is explained by B.N. Saraswati reiterating that the order by which both nature and culture are bound is the same. He takes a position that nature and culture do not constitute two distinct realities; rather, they coalesce with each other. It is, therefore, more appropriate to define this relationship by the expression, 'Nature **as** Culture' (which is the title of his paper) not 'Nature **and** Culture'. The forms of culture are subject to the fivefold order of 'origination', 'binding', 'interlocking' 'overlapping' and 'transcending' much like the elements of nature. This is most explicit among indigenous communities as the Santhals which thrive in the niche of nature. The vision of harmony between nature and Santhal culture in particular is rooted in the understanding that the people derive their design of life from the processes and phenomena of nature itself. One of the most evident of these and which comes out clearly in Nita Mathur's article is the cultivation and growth of plants. The laying of the seed in the womb of the earth and the emergence of a plant which bears seeds arrests the imagination of the people. Not surprising, therefore, the seed and womb emerges as a fundamental continuum in their thought and cognitive structure at empirical, physiological and metaphorical levels. The continuity between the apparently diverse dimensions of existence gets established. It is the seed of the plant world which gets transformed into the fertilizing fluid in the human body. Again, the seed is spoken about in verbal expressions as the *hā̄s dhuṛi* to mean first flowering of maturity on the one hand and the first leaves of a crop on the other which are both occasions of joy and celebration.

Another constituent of nature is animal. Subhra Bhattacharyya traces the relationship between animals and human beings, precisely Santhals, from their creation myth and goes on to explain the processes by which this relationship permeates class structure, marriage patterns and therapeutic practices. A new born animal is ceremonially incorporated into the family and looked after with much concern. Infact, a large corpus of Santhal myths and beliefs have to do with animals and people's own relationship with the animal world. Ajit Kūmar Aditya and Prasanta Chatterjee describe the mythological backdrop and system of beliefs against which their rituals and practices concerning domesticated and wild animals are contextualized. Ranging from reverence and worship to hunting, and from hunting to making artistic depictions, Santhals affirm their relationship at many levels and in many ways.

Animals are sacrificed on special occasions. Indrani Bhattacharyya (Chakraborty) mentions that the remains of any sacrifice to spirits of a village's outskirts are cooked and eaten outside the village itself for the fear of annoying them. Santhal cooking, whether of animals or plants, is regulated by space and time, and taste and flavour. The paper on Santhal concept of food brings to the fore the indigenous classification of food based on the mode of consumption, method of cooking, chief ingredients in cooking and taste and flavour. The people speak of food as 'fuel' that keeps the 'machinery' of the body in working order.

**Sound and Language :** Sound provides perhaps the first experience to all living beings — humans, animals and birds. Infants of many species are born with their eyes closed but ears wide open. On coming out of the darkness of the womb they let out a cry — the first sound. The sound which unites all cultures in terms of its pervasiveness is conceptualized and represented differently in different cultures. This makes for the richness of the composite traditions of music, dance, rituals, festivals and carnivals. More importantly, there is rich variegation in the articulation of sound in daily life and in patterns of language. Peter Pannke's paper on sounds from a Santhal village is based on recording of sounds of music, as also daily activities arranged in the form of a soundwalk through a Santhal village lasting from early hours of morning to late hours of night. In Santhal thought, the environment consists of sounds produced by striking together different objects, calls of animals and human speech and song. Certain sounds as the barking of a dog from the eastern direction, the cry of a vulture hovering over a village foretell unhappy events while harmony and synchrony between human and animal sounds as also those of nature foretells happiness and joy. The themes of cultural conception of sound and classification of birds and animals on the bases of the sounds they produce have been the centre point of Onkar Prasad's paper on Santhal classificatory approach to sound.

A large number of words in the language of Santhals derive from the natural sounds. This is illustrated in the paper of Khageswar Mahapatra complemented with Shyam Sundar Mohapatra's essay on the formation of Ol Chiki script and process of its transmission. The characters in Ol Chiki are derived from the physical environment and what surrounds the people — hills, rivers, trees, birds, bees, plough, sickle — the list is endless. Chaitanya Prasad Majhi, a Santhal scholar, reconstructs the cultural matrix in which the language and lifestyle of the people are embedded. It is the interrelationship between religion, beliefs, values and practices of a people which is significant here. In the larger context the language is based on experience and mundane concerns. The resonance of natural sounds in spoken words and pictographic characters of the script provide a glimpse into the mindset of the Santhals for whom nature exists as a self measured reality from which the people derive their design of living and patterns of language.

**Lifestyle and Worldview :** Lifestyle and worldview mark cultural identity. Lifestyle itself is abstracted from the web of relationships between human beings and the physical environment, among human beings themselves as also with plants and animals. In cultures, some of these relationships are sacrilized and constitute a part of the cosmological realm. One of the most appropriate examples of an interface between the gross or physical world and the cosmological world of the Santhals is the tradition of *jadupata* documented by Nilanjana Das (Saha). The *jadupatas* are paintings of men, women and children that are taken around by the practitioners — the *Jadupatuas* — in Santhal villages. In the house of a bereaved family they skilfully negotiate their skill and authority to communicate with the dead people.

The communication with those in the other world is not limited to ancestral beings or spirits of the dead but expands and enlarges to incorporate all the *bongas* — the general term for spirits. Sitakant Mahapatra elucidates the integrative and interactive relationship between Santhals and the *bongas* whom they always seem anxious to appease. There are *bongas* of the house, the sacred grove, the mountains, the forest. Infact, they are all pervasive and all permeating. All the major stages of agricultural operations are important occasions on which the *bongas* are invoked and worshipped to ensure that the crops do not fail. P.C. Hembram, another Santhal scholar complements this in highlighting the beliefs and rituals of the people which uphold the faith that all the components of the physical environment are abodes of spirits. Any disturbance in the order of nature or any kind of tampering with it evokes the wrath of these spirits. The interpersonal relationships, interactions between people, rituals and activities for subsistence are all undertaken within the framework of the norms of nature.

Evidently then, thought processes revolve around the sky, sun, moon, stars, clouds, rain, hail, wind, fire, dew, mist, earth, plants and all that amidst which they find themselves. S.K. Chakraborty explains that for the people, land which produces crop is the most important resource. The earth is regarded as mother goddess. It bears crops which sustain the people. Santhals are given to cultivation of rice. They also grow, among others, bananas. The endeavour of preparing the soil, manuring, laying the seeds, and harvesting the crop web together all the elements of nature because of which plants bear fruits and more seeds. It also provides the substratum from which their perspective of viewing the world is obtained.

This is taken up by N. Patnaik in mentioning that Santhals give countenance to the 'play principle' following which they seek to enjoy life to the fullest. Infact, all impositions that curtail their free will such as deadlines and time tables are rejected by them outright. The author explains that for the Santhal, happy life is one which is not constrained by ill-health and disease, conflicts, friction, resentment and more importantly by unpleasantness between human beings and the spirits. People spend their entire lives optimizing cordiality and togetherness between human beings, nature and spirits. In the wake of acculturation and modernization, the Santhal culture, much like that of other communities, is given to change. Conjoined with change are the attempts of people to uphold ethnic identity. Forces of change and resistance to change operate together. Sachchidananda guages the impact of increasing contact with people of other cultures, developmental programmes of the government and new technology on Santhal culture and worldview. It is argued that people have been able to safeguard the moral and social order and even avail themselves of the benefits accruing from acculturation. Herein, lies the strength of the culture making for its enrichment and continuity in all times to come.

Quintessentially, Santhals locate their lifestyle and worldview in cooperation, mutual care and love. The cultural expressions in nature, sound, language, creativity and sensitivity treat all life forms as sacred and respect them for what they are. Not only forms of life but even inanimate things and phenomena of nature are regarded as sacred. The sacredness is re-established in metaphors, rituals, songs, dance and everyday practices. This is the pristine, primal vision from which the new world order has much to learn.

**Nita Mathur**

# 1

# NATURE AS CULTURE
## The Vision of a Tradition

***Baidyanath Saraswati***

There are two incompatible maxims : *cultura ex cultura* and *cultura ex natura.* Both have given rise to what might be called the 'ladder mentality'. The ladder symbolizes a climb from simple to complex, from instinct to intelligence, from non-living to living, from less conscious to more conscious, from inorganic elements to plants to animals to humans, from savagery to civilization. In each case the world is pinned to a ladder of progressive development.

The aim of this presentation is to show that there is an existential connection between nature and culture. Man cannot live without nature, for he cannot live without spirit either. The ancients had 'seen' the invisible, the spiritual. Their initiatic lifestyle and thought followed the spirit of the natural world. That can still be seen in some parts of the world not in imitation of olden times but in continuation of the primal vision.

### The Transcendent Order of Nature

The Indian tradition has made a unique contribution to thought that characteristically looks inward upon the Universe. A splendid example of this is the Theory of Elements. The basic assumption in this is that, like the rest of the material world, man is made of

Elements which at death disintegrate and dissolve into nature. At the most general level there are nine Elements: Earth, Water, Fire, Air, Sky, Time, Directions, Mind and Soul. Of these the first five are called *bhuta* and the last four *dravya.* The gross and the subtle aspect of the Elements are recognized. The reality of the subtler plane is said to be responsible for the grosser plane, and at a higher level of realization the distinction between the gross and the subtle gets totally obliterated.

Elements of nature are subject to a fivefold order: origination, binding, interlocking, overlapping and transcending.

## ORIGINATION

Tribal cosmogony refers to a state of nothingness. In the beginning everything was Water, or Cloud, or nothing at all but two Eggs shining like gold. As the Eggs broke open, from one came the Earth, from the other the Sky. Metaphorically, when the Sky made love to Earth every kind of being was born.

## BINDING

Elements of nature constitute human and other forms, both individually and collectively. Each major organ is said to have its own builder. Head and ears are associated with Sky; neck and chest with Air; stomach with Fire; and body with Earth. Elements are known to have caused bio-social types. The ironsmiths relate themselves with Earth, carpenters with Water, coppersmiths with Fire, sculptors with Air, and goldsmiths with Sky.

## INTERLOCKING

Form and life are cross-linked. Metaphorically, Earth and Sky are Universal Parents. Fire and Air are brothers just as Water and Mist are brothers. Earth and Air, and Water and Fire are negatively linked, they have always been enemies. Air is the friend of Fire.

## OVERLAPPING

Elements have both personal (material) and universal (spiritual) attributes. Water and Egg, which appeared in the beginning, have a fundamental feature of sacredness. However, not all Elements are spiritually vibrant all the time, at all places. But they can be made so in a ritual way.

TRANSCENDING
Life transcends the limits of form. Death transcends all attributes of Elements, including the limits of temporality. There is no intrinsic disorder in nature. Dissolution is its integral aspect. Transcendence is the order of all orders. It is inviolable.

**The Natural Order of Culture**

Tribal myths deny the uniqueness of man in so far as his origin is concerned. Man is not unique even in the possession of knowledge. Primordial knowledge came to him from birds and animals. The priest of all creatures was born ahead of human beings. Cosmic Intelligence is the self-existent source of all knowledge.

Man lives on the Earth in the company of animals and spirits. Natural Elements are under the control of spirits. The spirits are everywhere. They are the invisible controller. They can be influenced only by the priest.

Rituals are performed in the sacred grove, the source of water, hill-tops, and mountain caves. Time for ritual is determined by the Sky, season, lunar changes, day-and-night, moments of natural calamity, etc. Ritual helps man to experience the rhythm of life. The performer of a ritual returns to the primordial state to reunite with the primal Elements, and to rejoice earthly existence. There are rituals involving group pantomimes of rolling in dust, acrobating in water, walking on burning embers, and swinging upside down on burning ashes. Such ritual acts affirm belief in the supernatural order.

Elements of nature have a veritable role in the making of a cultural person. Biologically, man is made up of Earth, Water, Fire, etc. Pigmentation, formation and function of the body tissues, sense organs, etc., are associated with the Five Elements. Psychologically also man is conditioned by the attributes of Elements. Human personality type is determined by biological time, beginning from the birth. Man of matter moves upward through a ritual process of socialization at different stages in life. Though sacerdotal in form, ritual establishes the importance of the earthly life and help organize a distinctive and coherent cultural pattern.

In this view, culture is conceived as natural projection of the inner self. The inner world merges into the outer world of Elements. Elements are not the created entities, they make the world by their own powers. Hence sacred.

**The Santhal Example**

The Santhals claim that the Elements originated in phases. Water, Earth and Sky came first, and subsequently Air and Fire. Man appeared as a ritual being tuned to nature. This is reflected in their categorical terms for space, time, object, person and action. These are deeply related in as much as they give the first meaning to their life and culture.

SPACE

The Santhal conception of space is simple but perfect in terms of their own experience and intuitive discovery of the immediate environment. The cosmic space is the spirit space. *Maran Buru* is the spirit who dwelt with the first Santhal. *Pargana bonga* is the spirit of the region. *Sima bonga* is the boundary spirit. *Manjhi Haram* is the spirit of the founder of the village. *Orak bonga* is the house spirit. *Bir bonga* is the forest spirit. *Jaher era* is the spirit of the sacred grove. *Dadi bonga* is the spring spirit.

TIME

While performing a ritual the Santhal experiences the space-time continuum. *Bir Sandra* is the time for seasonal hunting. *Bhinsar* is the time of dawn dancing. *Na-amke* is the famine time. *Mak-more* is the epidemic time. The ordering of time is based on nature's signal: on the appearance of the moon, on the blossoming of plants, on the fruiting of trees. The principal festival is celebrated in the spring. It is called *Sarhul,* the 'Feast of Sal Blossoms', also known as the 'Marriage of the Earth'. If circumstances demand, the time is determined by direct divination.

OBJECT

A distinction is made between the natural object and the constructed object. But both are sacred, effective. Earth, water, fire, tree, flowers and mountains are ritual objects. *Ranu,* a ferment made of roots and bark, and *Tumdak,* the dancing drum, are also sacred.

PERSON

The Santhal view of person is not limited to man. A distinction is made between the cosmic person and the physically manifest being. Among the cosmic persons there are: *Thakur Jiu,* the creator; *Bidhi,* the controller and allocator of soul and sex of a female child; *Bidhanta,* the controller of destiny and allocator of soul and sex of a male child; *Jom Raja,* the King of the Dead; *Divi,* the goddess. As evident, these heavenly beings are not indigenous to the Santhal world. The real cosmic person is *bonga.* The nature or the degree of reality of *bonga* is known by its spiritual presence and power. There are *bongas* of festivals: *Baha bonga,* the spirit of *Baha* flower festival; *Mag bonga,* the spirit of *Mag* festival. Their power springs from latency to action. *Saket* is the tutelary spirit of a medicine man. *Moreko-Turuiko,* the Five-Six (*Moreko* means five, male, and *Turuiko* means six, female), are the spirits who were the first to organize the Santhal way of life. *Maran Buru* or *Lita* is the greatest of all spirits. Among the beings known by physical presence, *Hor* (man) himself is a potential expression of cosmic power and cosmic power itself is an expression of an even more subtle, more intangible, order known as the field of *bonga. Naeke,* the village priest, derives his power from the *bonga. Ojha,* the medicine man, is also empowered by the *bonga.* So also *dihri,* the hunt master; *bhogla,* the priest of the hook-swinging festival; and *jan,* the soothsayer. *Hor* is a region-bound concept which stands for 'man'. *Hor* also means 'ways'. Thus it is said: *Hor,* the man, is always in search of a *hor* (way). The term *Sanat-Hor* means 'pure and honest man'. *Doho-Hor* means 'traditional mandates handed down from one generation to the next'. There are other related terms such as *Sari-Panja,* search for truth; *Sarna,* the divine altar, sacred grove; and *Sari-Sarna,* the religion of the sacred grove. Both spiritually and socially, *Hor* is related to plants, trees and animals. There are several totemic clans such as Grass, Betel Palm, Areca Nut, *Panjan* Tree, Dense Jungle, Mountain, Hawk, Pigeon, Crow, Wild Goose, *Nilgai,* Sheep, Buffalo, Deer, Breed Pigs with large tusks, Cobra, Lizard, Tortoise, Fish and Crab. It is only with reference to these that a social-and-human personality type is determined.

ACTION

The Santhals act in a ritual way. They have developed a fourfold ritual language that helps communication with nature and spirit :

(a) Esoteric World

*Jharni,* Invocation; *Bakhen,* invocatory songs; *Binti,* songs of cosmology; *Hital,* songs of creator; *Don Seren,* songs of wedding; *Kudum,* riddles.

(b) Gestures

*Enec,* dance; *Danta,* the *Sohrae* festival dance; *Kulhi Enec,* street dance; *Lagre,* the dance of enjoyment; *Golwari,* dance with pantomime gestures; *Kanta Pata,* rolling or walking on thorns; *Nian Pata,* fire walking; *Ugra Pata,* hanging head down on fire; *Uda Pata,* rotating on horizontal plane; *Johar,* gestures of greeting.

(c) Sound

Significance is attahced to flute and drum. Dull thudding of a *Tumdak* at the annual hunt and *Der Der, Deper Deper* shouting during *Bitlaha* dance hold in potential all the power of nature.

(d) Critical Action

*Oteili* is a ceremonial act connected with land. *Erok* or *Eroh* is an act of worship for sowing seeds. *Sura Sagen Mahamane* is a ritual act of invigorating a slow-growing crop. *Asadia* is a worship for weeding operations. *Jantral* is a worship for protection of crops from birds, *Janthar* is a festival of the first fruit. *Gundali* is a festival of eating the first millet. *Nim Dak Mandi* is a cleaning ceremony. *Sid* is an initiation rite. *Bitlaha* is punitative mass gathering for major offences.

## Conclusion

The ancients had built their initiatic culture entirely around nature. Their way of life followed subtle insights. They actualized those insights as more comprehensible thoughts. Thoughts became more structured by categorical terms. The categorical terms gave a ritual language and language led to material forms of expression. The ritual language paves the way of life, keeps the Santhals ahead with nature of which they are an inseparable part. Maintaining this attunement with nature shows the *Hor* to resonate with the world filled with the spirit. In Santhal cosmology, metaphorically, culture is an Inverted Tree with Roots upward and Branches beneath. The pattern of life appears as a tangible actualization of an unseen reality. That Inverted Tree (the *peepal*, the *vata*) stands in their sacred grove where the Five-Six, the *Maran Buru, Gosai era* and *Manjhi Haram* are invoked.

How can, then, nature be separated from culture. Truly speaking, the Santhal *Sari-Sarna* is the culture of the 'sacred grove'. The Santhals have understood the basic relatedness of nature and culture, without the imposition of a theory based on creation (in the Christian sense) or evolution (in the Darwinian sense). The Theory of Elements disproves both creationism and evolutionism. *Bonga* is not God or god, it is a creative spirit of the world.

Briefly, the traditional Santhal culture is the prime extant example of an initiatic lifestyle that has proved its capacity to integrate harmoniously the natural and the supernatural worlds.

### BIBLIOGRAPHY

Biswas, P. C., 1956, *Santals of the Santal Parganas,* Delhi : Bharatiya Adimjati Sevak Sangh.

Bodding, P. O., 1942, *Traditions and Institutions of the Santals,* Oslo : A. W. Broggers Boktrykkeri.

Hembram, P. C., 1988, *Sari-Sarna (Santhal Religion),* Delhi : Mittal Publications.

# 2

# SANTHAL CONCEPT OF WOMB AND SEED

*Nita Mathur*

---

Ever since anthropologists, set out to explore oral cultures in India, the inadequacy of pervading concepts, paradigms and theories has been realized. Derived from database that did not take cognizance of Indian, what in anthropological parlance are understood as 'tribal communities', they seem to be ill-tailored for cultural reality here. This appears more acute to 'insider anthropologists' who belong to oral cultures and understand them most closely. It is, therefore, essential to evolve alternatives and reconstruct paradigms that will foster comprehension of these cultures in fullness.

The lifestyle, self-conscious awareness and identity of a people is nurtured and sustained by the continual flux between concepts, symbols, images and their interpretation in cultural systems. These are very well articulated in architecture, painting, music, dance, theatre and aspects of fairs and festivals constituting the broad spectrum of creative and critical representations. The problem then is one of identifying the interconnections within and between the many dimensions of nature, ecology, knowledge system, traditional technologies and artistic manifestations constituting the cradle of culture in which human beings find themselves. The search for solution is a journey beyond intellection into the realms of indigenous knowledge systems, vision and basic philosophy as undercurrents of empiricism. These make for rituals and cultural practices at the manifest level and mindset of the people at the abstract level conjoining the material with the spiritual, subtle with gross and outer with inner.

At the conceptual plane, there are identifiable themes that cut across the depths of time and spread of space. They emerge repeatedly in mundane patterns of living, rituals, aesthetic creativity and thought processes. In fact, the original nexus of fundamental concepts generates the complex webwork of symbols with ramifications in the language, linguistic categories and vocabulary. This keeps the entire cultural equipage vibrant ensuring its continuity through generations.

More specifically, the Santhals understand the internal representations by what they see 'out there'. The semblance between processes of nature and articulations developed in the culture bear this out. The chief concern of the Santhals given to cultivation for subsistence is with making the most of the land and seed. Evidently, the seed and womb constitute the centre point of cosmology, imagery in beliefs and rituals that go a long way in developing their social organization and life functions . In this paper, which is born out of a project undertaken by me at the Indira Gandhi National Centre for the Arts, I seek to reconstruct the Santhal concept of womb and seed from their language, beliefs, rituals and life philosophy at three levels : empirical, physiological and metaphorical.

## The Empirical Level

At the empirical level, the seed is the fertilizing fluid from which organic life derives and the foodgrain which sustains it. The earth is a large womb in which the seed gets embedded. The growth and development of the seed is related with the fertility of the soil. The farmer who prepares the earth, sows the seed, looks after the saplings and harvests the grain recognizes most closely the relationship between the seed and the womb.

In one of the earliest attempts to get something out of the soil, it is likely that Santhals cleared a patch of ground. Here they scattered the seeds. It is said that formerly the Santhals did not plough the land at all. They simply dropped the seeds in small holes made along a steep hillside. The seeds spread by rainwater flowing down the hill (Biswas, 1956). In the present day, however, the Santhals select a site for cultivation, clear it of weeds and other vegetation. Then they surround it with ridges. The earth is prepared to receive the seed. It is levelled and ploughed arduously several times before laying the seeds and transplanting the rice saplings. From morning to evening men and women work in the fields. The whole year is spent away in ploughing, sowing, transplanting, harvesting and threshing.

Some of the primary rituals in the Santhal life celebrate the rice (seed) - earth (womb) relationship . The rituals also reflect the people's anxieties regarding the eco-cycle, fertility of the soil and rhythms of nature upon which the growth of the seed and its maturation depend. This is tied up with the benignity of the *bongas* or spirits. The argicultural rituals, in essence, invoke the benevolence of the *bongas.*

Sometime between June and July, the seed is sown in the earth at the *Erok* festival. The village priest sacrifices fowls in the sacred grove and invokes the *bongas* in the following verses (cf. Mahapatra, 1992:175):

> Our obeisance to you, Mother Jaher Era.
> On the occasion of Erok festival we offer you
> young fowls, and freshly husked rice.
> Accept it in pleasure.
>
> We pray to you :
> For every seed we sow let there be twelve
> And let not disease attack them.
> If they attack, please subdue them.
> Do not allow weeds and grass to grow among our crops.
> Do not allow diseases and misfortune to befall our village,
> Bring us the rain-bearing clouds in plenty.
> Bring them in time.
>
> Let the earth be green with our crops,
> Let there be no hindrance to our movements,
> Let there prevail among us
> The spirit of mutual love and goodwill

The impending fear of anything that will thwart the process of germination is allayed by making sacrifices and appeasing the spirits. The people collectively pray for water, rains and favourable conditions that foster the sprouting of the seeds. This includes the well-being of the cultivators and their families who take care of the seedlings when they come up. They communicate with the *bongas* through the language of ritual and incantation obtained from the so-much-ness of life.

The *Erok* festival is followed by *Hariar Sim* between July and August when the rice has begun to sprout. Fowls are sacrificed and the *bongas* are invoked again for the paddy to grow green and full. The maturing crop is ceremonially gathered in November-December and offered to the *bongas* at the sacred grove as part of the *Janthar* ritual. The village priest sacrifices a pig or ram and says to the *bongas*, "Be greeted then, Father my Thakur, Pargana, in the name of the Janthar we are giving thee, handing thee sacrifices, offerings; consequently we shall eat, take it into our mouth, do not let stomach ache, headache be created, be formed; in the ricefields, on the threshing-floors we shall reap, we shall thresh; mayest thou make it fertile, make it rich; mayest thou add to it, multiply it; rat and field mouse will attack it; these also thou will restrain, keep back. Father, my Thakur" (Bodding, 1942:136). The first gathering of rice grains is distributed among the villagers.

The asking for plentitude and prosperity gives way to distinctive expression of gratitude to the beings of the other world after the harvest in December-January. With large heaps of rice, the Santhals make merry for five days in the *Sohrae* festival. Fowls are sacrificed, rice-beer is brewed and more importantly, fertility of cows is awakened through blessings. Amidst eating, drinking, singing and dancing, the Santhals even step outside the circumference of moral codes of behaviour. This may result in adultery. The offence is, however, punished less severely if it is committed in the period of *Sohrae* than at any other time.

The many stages of rice cultivation strengthening, reinforcing and re-affirming the seed-earth relationship brings together members of the community from time to time. Occasions such as these provide an opportunity to participate in agricultural events with a sense of togetherness and concern. The time for hard labour on the one hand and complete rejoicing on the other are both determined by the crop cycle. In fact, the lifestyle of the Santhals, also true of other agricultural communities, revolves around the small grain of rice and the entire sequence of events related with its cultivation.

**The Physiological Level**

According to Santhal cosmology, the potential of life is contained in the seed. In the beginning there was nothing but an expanse of water. One day, *Thakur* — the Lord, determined to create the Universe, made two birds out of the dirt on his shoulders. He infused life by breathing on them. The birds were restless, for, there was no place to perch. *Thakur* brought out the earth from under the waters and put in the seed for trees and vegetation on which the birds could build their nests. The birds soon laid two eggs from which were born the first man and woman. Evidently, the source of both, plant and human life, is the seed.

Following the cultural theory, there are two kinds of human seed — the male and the female, both mobile and potent. Drawing the complete theory of conception detailed here from Archer (1974), it may be mentioned that the man's seed obtains from blood and marrow which trickles down a vein into the organ. There it is made into semen and gathers in a little bag. When this gets filled up, the entire body is filled with inexhaustible strength. In a woman's body, the seed is formed in the womb. Much like the male seed, it collects in a tiny bag.

The basic rhythm in the woman's body prepares the womb for conception. In the first two days, the seed is simply thrown out with the flow. The womb is best prepared to receive and retain the seed on the last day on which, as they say, 'the flower ends'. This is a meaningful expression, for, the ending of flower marks the development of the fruit. The day a woman's flower ends, the man's seed may enter without any resistance. It easily finds the 'flower's root' from which her blood comes.

It is said that at the time of conception, a woman's seed comes before the man's seed and smoothens the way for it to glide in. Alternatively, a woman's seed comes from one side and the man's seed from the other. The two seeds mingle and change into blood, get encased in a shell and grow bigger. In four months time child forms and *jivi* or soul swimming in the blood settles in it. In due course, the head sprouts and eyes appear. After this, the body develops and arms, legs differentiate. The gender is determined by the *jivi* itself . The one bestowed by *bidhi* — the mythological feminine fate writer — is responsible for the birth of the girl child while that bestowed by *bidhanta* — bidhi's male counterpart — is responsible for the birth of a boy child. The womb provides warmth and sustenence for growth. Later, the mother nourishes the children with her milk. She is referred to as the 'milk tree' by them.

The Santhals look forward to the birth of children after marriage. The power to grant life lies with *Thakur Jiu*. A woman is not able to conceive if 'her child's house (womb) is dirty', or a witch has inverted the womb and blackened the blood, or else the man's seed is weak. Worse is the situation in which a *bonga* seduces the woman in the guise of a man. His fluid renders conception from human beings impossible. Men and women remain anxious to please the *Thakur* and *bongas* to avert barrenness. One of the ways in which this is done effectively is the *Janam Karam* ritual. The *Karam* tree is believed to inhere special flowers to increase one's progeny and wealth. The *Janam Karam* ritual celebrates the chance appearance of *Karam* seedlings on a man's land. At the outset, the villagers protect the seedlings by winding cotton thread around the twigs that surround it. A series of rituals are performed. The village priest gently digs the earth around it and the man pulls it out with much care. He places it in a pot which is carried in the lap of his wife to their own shrine. The *Dangua Karam* is performed once in five years for early marriage of eligible boys and girls of the village. The sequence of rituals is followed by women bringing out cucumbers covered with paddy leaves in a winnowing fan. These are shown to people around saying, "here are the babies". This is clearly the simulation of birth by propitiating the *Karam tree* and *bongas*. It is believed to enhance fertility so that conception and birth are not delayed.

According to Bodding (1927) the Santhals believe that the human body is constituted of *sirs* or muscles and *sinews* or nerves, arteries and veins. The blood is formed in the *sirs.* A large number of *sirs* meet at the dorsal side of the body. The food that we eat first reaches the stomach where it is diluted. It finally turns into blood through intermittent stages. The body functions so long as the internal processes are normal. When any part gets out of tune with others, the body comes to a standstill till it is attended to. The Santhals uphold the belief that the cause of disease and death, in the final, is the anger of evil spirits, witches and sometimes the dead people. They, therefore, have to take measures for counteracting the inimical influence of these powers through propitiation, appeasement or even confrontation. The medicine man seeks to gather the disease at one point of the body by way of incantations and assistance of special *bongas*. This is then removed from the body by biting and sucking. He may drive away the disease by reciting a *mantar* or sacred verse and blowing over the patient's body from head to toe. Alternatively, the human body is shielded by a *mantar* against the impending danger of being afflicted with a disease.

*Banjhi* or barrenness is also cured by exorcising evil spirits. The husband and wife carrying an earthen pot full of water on the head are taken to the end of the village street. The medicine man clears hurdles by passing a mottled fowl around them thrice. The woman sits on a stool and the water from the pot is poured on her. She changes the clothes and leaving the wet ones there itself she walks towards her home without looking back. The man also reaches home after breaking the earthen pot. Later, the medicine man gives an ear of paddy to the woman. She carefully tucks it in the front fold of her cloth. After a short while, she looks at it to count how many of the grains remain intact. This indicates the number of children who would survive. Then he gives the medicine reciting specific verses (Bodding, ibid). The pot full of water in this ritual represents the fertile womb. The water is regarded as life-giving. The pouring out of water on the barren woman is an act of bestowing fertility on her. The empty earthen pot representing the infertile womb is appropriately broken into pieces.

## The Metaphorical Level

The reference point of knowledge in the Santhals as also those of other oral cultures is the human life world. The vocabulary, cognitive and conceptual categories derive from the real world and empirical reality. They are distinguished by a way of life which is participatory and, experiential rather than distanced from the environment and various forms of life; cohesive and coherent rather than fragmentary and itemized; and empirical rather than abstract and analytical.

It is not surprising, therefore, that a pregnant woman is spoken of as 'one who has collected a bundle of seeds'. This ties up with their notion of conception as the coming together of male and female seeds. The collection of a 'bundle of seeds' to mean pregnancy explains the process as also the physical condition of distension. In corollary, the woman is a kind of container of seeds much like the earth itself . The woman and the earth both nourish the seeds in their bodies till they mature. In coming out or sprouting, the seedlings break apart the surfaces. In line with this is the metaphor of seed and seedling for children.

According to a Santhal narration, once upon a time their ancestors cleared the jungle. They kept *iṛi (Panicum crus-galli)* and *erba* (*Setaria italica*) seeds in gourd shells. Much to their surprise the *iṛi* seeds yielded *erba* plants and *erba* seeds yielded *iṛi* plants (Bodding, op. cit). In Santhal thought there is a close correspondence between seed of plants and that of human beings. The gourd shell here represents the womb in which seeds are contained. The mixing of two kinds of seeds replays, so to say, the process of procreation. Santhal men and women often ask each other as to how many *iṛi* and *erba* seeds have shot into ears to mean daughters and sons respectively.

The term for the after-birth placenta is *awar*, figuratively used for old clothes especially those of a bridegroom. These are, naturally, to be changed. The conjoining of birth with marriage is explained by the new life, new situation that both, birth and marriage, lead to. Another term for placenta is *baha* which is also the flower festival celebrated during February-March when the Sal tree blossoms.

As the seedlings are born and are ready for transplanting, men and women sway in joy addressing them in songs as their own children imbued with consciousness. The following are few songs, cited from Archer (op. cit : 22).

I. Wealth, Wealth,
O Mother Wealth

Where was your birth?
I was born
In a splash of rain.

2. The paddy is weeping,
The paddy is asking,
When will be my wedding ?
When the water of the sky
Drenches the earth,
Then will be your wedding,

3. Wealth, Wealth
Where is your mother ?
Who is your father ?
My mother and father
Are rain and wind,
My milk is water trickling.

Here, seedlings as children are associated with prosperity, auspiciousness and happiness. The sky is the male principle, earth is the female principle and water represents the semen or life principle. The process of transplantation involving change of residence is, in fact, the wedding of the children — an event they look forward to. The aspirations of parents-cultivators is that the crops come up full and complete.

The word *dhuṛi* connotes the first flowering of maturity. In another context, it refers to the first leaves of the crop. These are occasions for joy and celebration. Any failure is a matter of serious concern. The terms for both stunted paddy and, short children is *duluc' dupuc', bagar gaṭhia* and *ạli*. By the same token is the term *her her* for bare trunk in the vegetal world and human barrenness or the cessation to bear children. Maturation or growing old is likened to ripening of fruits expressed by the term *ararao*. Finally, the ripened fruit withers; new seeds are sown and the cycle begins. At the time of death when the body is consigned to flames, the ash is collected at one place while the remaining area is cleaned. Culshaw (1949) mentions that the area is plastered with cowdung and parched rice is sprinkled. This is spoken of as 'sowing' the rice. The sequence of birth-growth-death and regeneration gets completed. This is eventually what life and living is all about.

The Santhal knowledge is not confined to the seed and the earth but through it expands to embrace the entire world and also the celestial-transcendental realms. Their worldview and understanding of the world are derived from a sense of fullness and personal experience. The womb-seed continuum so conspicuous in the world of plants and animals emerges repeatedly in the Santhal cognitive paradigms. The challenge is to gauge the vast cultural reality and work out models for understanding cultures in their entirety.

## REFERENCES

Archer, W. G., 1974, *The Hill of flutes : Life, Love and Poetry in Trial India,* London: George Allen & Unwin Ltd.

Biswas, P. C., 1956, *Santals of Santal Parganas,* Delhi : Bhartiya Adimjati Sevak Sangh.

Bodding, P. O., 1927, *Studies in Santal Medicine and Connected Folklore,* Calcutta : Asiatic Society of Bengal.

____________, 1942, *Traditions and Institutions of the Santals,* Oslo : A. W. Broggers Boktrykkeri.

Mahapatra, S. K., 1992, *Unending Rhythms : Oral Poetry of Indian Tribes,* New Delhi: Inter-India Publications.

Culshaw, W.K., 1949, *Tribal Heritage : A Study of the Santals,* London : Lutterworth Press.

# 3

# MAN AND ANIMAL RELATIONSHIP

***Subhra Bhattacharyya***

---

Animals have been in close association with man since prehistoric times as revealed by the rock art and cave paintings in which animal figures dominate. Paintings depicting hunting scenes were probably designed to bring luck to the hunter or mark respect to the spirit of the prey. Apart from the provision of food and clothing, animals were connected with religious beliefs and practices, particularly among the people who lived by hunting or by raising flocks and herds or by cultivation. They were worshipped as supernatural beings. It is also said that man learnt a lot by imitating animals, as Saraswati (1991) puts it, "primordial knowledge came to him from birds and animals". Making of huts, weaving and expressions of love and sorrow are said to have been learnt from birds and animals.

We need animals for our food, or as a help in our work. Some of us hunt animals and organize animal races and fights for amusement. These, however, are not the only aspects of our relationship with animals. The mind of each one of us, no matter what life we may lead or what tradition we may have been brought up in, has been moulded to some extent by contact with these fellow creatures — animals. The reverence of man for these enigmatic beings which surround him is so great that he projects them as it were into the heavens — the Great Bear, the Great Dog. They appear as the dog - star, the lion, scorpion, or sheep shining in the zodiac or among the constellations.

## Creation

The Santhal myth of creation of the world differs slightly from those of other Chota Nagpur tribes. We begin with the creation of seven primeval animals by God, then refer to these animals creating land, followed by the emergence of the first man and woman and of mankind.

The Santhals believe that originally the world was filled with water and God had the problem in the creation of land — the opposite of water. He created seven animals — crab, crocodile, alligator, eel, prawn, earthworm and tortoise. All the animals can operate in water as well as on land. They connect the two opposed elements. Out of the seven animals, six failed to create land. Only the earthworm was successful and for seven days and seven nights he ate the earth at the bottom of the water and excreted it on the back of the tortoise who was swimming on the top. The tortoise anchored himself on both sides firmly and brought the earth up. Thus land was shaped and it shakes (earthquakes) when the tortoise moves. This Santhal myth is unique in a way that it ascribes the creation of the world to these ambiguous animals specially the earthworm and the tortoise.

God next created two heavenly birds — *Has* and *Hasil* — out of his hair. Both these birds rose to the sky. They were not destroyed as they mediated the opposition of the elements — heaven and earth. They flew below the sun and above the earth, thus making contact with both the worlds. After flying for several days they built a nest on the earth to lay eggs. They laid two cosmic eggs, out of which hatched two creatures — a human male and a human female. Thus two heavenly birds giving birth to two earthly human beings becomes significant in Santhal life. They regard these two birds as their ancestors from whom *Pilcu Haram* and *Pilcu Budhi* (the earthbound children of heavenly descent) descended.

Both these myths — creation of the world and of mankind — refer to the animals and birds as ancestors. The Santhal concept of life thus begins with animals. The clans are named after animals.

**Totemism**

*Pilcu Haram* and *Pilcu Budhi* gave birth to seven sons and seven daughters who in turn married each other and formed seven exogamous clans. In course of time five more groups were formed. A total of 12 clans is found among the Santhals. They are *Hansdak, Murmu, Hembram, Soren, Kisku, Marndi, Tudu, Baske, Besra, Chore, Pauria* and *Bedea.* Each of these clans derived its name from plant and animal species. A kinship or sacred relationship is believed to link these clans and their respective totems.

The Santhals do not strictly believe in descent from the totemic animals, but indicate that the totems have some connection with the birth or deeds of the ancestors of the clan. *Hansdak* clan members claim to be of the highest status as they have derived the name of their clan from the first ancestors. The term *Has* designates a goose while *dak* in Santhali means water. This clan is, therefore, linked to the original state of the world and to the first ancestors. It is the most senior among all the clans of the Santhals since it is related to the myth of creation. Moreover, the swan or goose is not just a water animal. It builds nests on earth and walks on land, and also flies in the sky. The members of the *Hansdak* clan too link themselves closely to these four elements which are regarded superior to the others for they claim to rule over the four elements.

Next in order are the *Murmus* who are represented by the *nilgai* or the antelope. The myth of origin of this clan speaks of the antelope as the first animal to be hunted by the ancestors of the clan and therefore the first animal to be sacrificed by the Santhals. From then onwards the Sánthals became fond of hunting and eating the flesh of animals. The antelope being purely a land animal is responsible for destruction among the Santhals as opposed to the swan who combines the four elements and stands for humanity and creation of human beings.

The *Hansdak* and the *Murmu* are the two superior clans of the Santhal tribe. Ancient literature suggests they did not intermarry (Biswas, 1956) and are believed to have consanguinal relationship. The *Hansdaks* are given the status of advisers and the *Murmus* are the priests.

The *Kiskus* have kingfisher bird as their totem and come third in hierarchy. They are regarded as kings and are given the royal status. *Hembrams* are fourth in order and have betel nut as their totem. It is believed that the ancestor of the *Hembram* clan was born with a betel nut string around his waist. There are also those who believe that their ancestor was actually born under a betel nut tree. The *Hembrams* represent nobility and truthfulness like the betel nut which is totally hard and solid.

*Marndis* are linked with grass or a type of weed and are traders. The *Sorens* are soldiers or warriors and are linked to the constellation of stars. The *Tudus* are musicians and have accepted owl as their totem. *Baskes* are cooks and associated with stale rice. They are believed to have offered stale rice to the gods and are thus prohibited from eating it themselves. *Bedeas* have sheep as their totem and are beleived to have no personality of their own much like the animal they rever. They are not found in the present day. Lastly are the *Paurias* and *Chores* who have pigeons and lizards respectively as their totems. Their ancestors probably killed only pigeons and lizards during an annual hunt. It is found in most of the cases that the only animals the clan members could hunt were made their totem which perhaps restricted them from endangering the species.

So strong are their feelings towards these totemic species that they respect them as their own clan members. If any of the clan member sees a dead totem, he observes the death rituals. The more important taboo is on marrying or entering into sexual relations with the members of the same totem group. Eating or harming the totem is prohibited. Clan names and totems are linked (Table 1).

**Table 1 :** Clan names and Totems

| | Clan Name | Totem | Element |
|---|---|---|---|
| 1. | *Hansdak* | swan | water, land, earth and heaven |
| 2. | *Murmu* | antelope | land |
| 3. | *Kisku* | kingfisher | heaven and earth |
| 4. | *Hembram* | betel nut | earth (upper) |
| 5. | *Marndi* | weed | earth (low) |
| 6. | *Soren* | constellation pleiades | heaven (upper) |
| 7. | *Tudu* | owl | heaven |
| 8. | *Baske* | stale rice | earth |
| 9. | *Besra* | hawk | heaven |
| 10. | *Bedea* | sheep | land |
| 11. | *Pauria* | pigeon | heaven |
| 12. | *Chore* | lizard | earth |

Preffer (1984) has explained the relationship between totems and clans in new light. According to him, old literature mentions restrictions in marriage between certain clans. The reasons lie in the nature of the totems and the elements they are connected with. In the first place, marriages are forbidden between water and land, i.e. swan (*Hansdak*) and antelope (*Murmu*). It is restricted between 'lower heaven' and 'lower earth', i.e. kingfisher and weed (*Kisku* and *Marndi*), also between 'upper earth' (*Hembram*) and 'upper heaven' (Soren). Secondly, marriages are prohibited between the three heavenly birds (owl, hawk and pigeon). The totems also define the relationship between the consumer and consumed. Rice is eaten by the pigeon who is the prey of the hawk along with the lizard and this lizard is also hunted by the owl. Therefore, initially the *Chores* did not marry with *Besras* and *Tudus*. These restrictions are not followed any more and marriages take place between all clan members.

Each of these clans is further divided into several sub-clans; each one upholds a distinctive myth and set of customs that differentiates it from the other, including kinds of food taken, ornaments worn and worship of spirits and deities. Even sacrifices during *Sohrae* or *Bandua* (a ritual observed to thank the deities and cattle after harvest), vary from one sub-clan to another. The names of the sub-clans are also derived from plants and animals. Out of the 16 sub-clans that were available in the area, nine trace their origin to certain animals. For example, *Chilbinda-Hansdak* derived its name from the ancestor who killed an eagle, *Jihu-Hansdak* from *jihu* or babbler bird, and *Kada* or *Karwar - Hansdak* from buffalo. It is said that the ancestor of *Kada-Hansdak* killed a buffalo to serve guests in a feast since the meat which had been cooked for them was not enough. *Sole-Hembrams* do not eat eels as it is beleived that their ancestors had been saved by a eel who ferried them over the flood river on its back. *Somal* or *Man-Sorens* have a species of deer as their totem. *Dantela-Hembrams* are so called because they rear pigs with large tusks for making sacrifice. The *Kahu-Besras* are prohibited to kill crows. *Kekra-Marndis* have crabs as their totems and *Nag-Kistens* have the hooded cobra.

The totem exercises a powerful influence on the habits of the Santhals. For a Santhal, killing of one's totem is equivalent to killing a member of his own clan. The clan members have brotherly feelings among themselves.

**Animal World**

In the Santhal pantheon there are animals appearing from the sky or shining as stars. They beleive in a day-horse (white horse with wings) who wanted to destroy the first human male and female when they were born. This heavenly day-horse stood as a destroyer of humankind. A dog — terrestrial being — appeared, and stood against the unfamiliar destroyer from the heaven. The day-horse is beleived to be an agent of the sun and the dog of the ancestors. This dog shines as a dog-star in the sky and stands as a saviour of mankind.

There is another myth about the creation of the *saptarishi* — the constellation of seven stars or the Great Bear. It is believed that after the death of the first ancestors of the Santhals — *Pilcu Haram* and *Pilcu Budhi* — their seven sons could not find any place on the earth to bury their parents. So, they laid them on a cot *(parkom)* made of bamboo and reached the heaven. The spirits of their parents were very pleased with the sons and wanted to be with them forever so they turned them into stars. This set of seven stars is also called *budhi parkom* meaning, 'their mother's cot'.

Santhals believe in the *Baghut bonga* or the spirit of tiger. They worship *Baghut* for the welfare of the villagers as well as the domesticated animals specially the cattle. *Baghut* worship is also common among the people who are hunter gatherers. They believe that sacrifices to the *Baghut* protect them from the dangers of the forest.

They also believe in the transmigration of souls into the bodies of beasts. This shows their way of recognizing the original relationship between the two living beings. It is believed that a drunk person would be born as a pig, a wicked one as a snake, a cruel one as a tiger and so on.

The Santhals broadly classify animals into three categories : first, the domesticated varieties and those that are sacrified to the deities, viz., cows, buffaloes, pigs, rabbits, goat, sheep, fowls, other birds etc., second, the smaller non-domesticated edible animals, but these are not offered to the deities : porcupine, mongoose, squirrels, snakes, frogs, rats, monkeys, etc; third, in the lowest category, are the animals whose flesh is neither eaten nor sacrificed but are beleived to be sacred and are feared : dogs, cats, tigers, elephants, horses, etc. Hard economic conditions force many people to offer clay figures of these animals as symbolic of the sacrifice of live ones. They also classify animals into domesticated *(rohoy)* and wild *(ayejtke)* varieties and birds into flying *(uddakkanah)* and non-flying *(dahakanah),* sometimes also into benevolent and malevolent kinds.

Though the Santhals are not directly concerned with all the animals of the forest for their day-to-day subsistence activities, they are quite familiar with their behaviour and activities. Ferocious animals, they believe, are not dangerous till they are disturbed or harmed. The fear of spirits of the killed animals seeking revenge for their death, lurks in people's minds. Sacrifices are made to appease these spirits. Goats and fowls are sacrificed on the annual hunt. The one who hits an animal first, whether it is killed or not, has a right over the animal, but he must give certain parts to others and must divide what is left with the men of his own village, keeping only certain parts to himself. On other hunts where only men of one village participate, all the participants get an equal share of a hunted animal including the dog who accompanies the hunters. When the men are out for hunt none of the villagers, that is, the children or the women, are allowed to kill any animal in the village till the hunters have returned, as this is believed to help achieve success in the hunt. The nature of intake of the hunt differs from one sub-clan to another. The meat of the animals is cooked outside the house and not taken into the house in which a woman is pregnant nor does any family member take the meat of the hunted animal away.

The Santhals are well versed in the art of hunting. They can judge the presence of an animal by seeing a hole or a cave, the direction of their movement, and can even bring down running animals or flying birds. Some of the animals, e.g. peacock, mongoose, hare, monkey, are brought home alive and are kept as pets. The Santhal children enjoy killing small animals as frogs, rats, garden lizards and birds. This is their favourite pastime. They often mercilessly stone down these creatures. Such children, especially boys, are regarded to be brave and make their parents proud. This shows that children are reared to be good hunters from the very young age. Nevertheless, the Santhals have a respect for all animals, live or dead. They never touch an animal with their legs for fear of making the spirits angry; a small portion is always offered to the supernatural deities before the hunt is shared.

Though the Santhals enjoy hunting wild animals, they are kind to the domesticated ones. Owning animals brings honour and prestige to a Santhal family. Sometimes a person is referred to by the types and number of animals owned by him or by people in the neighbouring village. The task of rearing animals is a joint responsibility of all the members of a family. Adults treat and take care of them as their own offsprings and the children befriend them easily. Once an animal is born or brought (from market or as bride price or gift) into a household, it becomes a part of the family. A new animal (eg. cattle) is initiated into the family by the application of turmeric and oil by an elderly woman on its horns, forehead and hoofs. A newly born animal is as much welcome to them as a human child. It is bestowed special care and attention by all the members of the family, specially children. The mother animal is taken care of by the women and not milked for at least a month. Earlier, cattle were never milked by Santhals as they beleived that they would be cursed by the calves and also because the Santhals do not want to deprive the young ones of their mother's care.

Diseases of these domesticated animals remain matter of concern of the Santhals principally because of the economic loss they bring. They have an inherent knowledge about the diseases the animals suffer from and usẹ indigenous medicines, usually made from plant extracts. They even offer sacrifices and make vows to the spirits of offerings for keeping the animals free from diseases all year through. This reveals their concern for these dumb creatures who, according to them, are more dear than their own lives.

The Santhals domesticate animals for various purposes. Dogs are owned by almost all the families for hunting and helping to catch pigs and fowls. Oxen and buffaloes are used in agricultural activities and for transport. They often use buffalo-carts to travel to neighbouring villages. Goats and sheep are reared for trade, sacrifices, and food. Pigs and fowls are also kept in large numbers for the same purpose. Fat of pigs is used to lubricate cart wheels. Cats are often found in a village, but are not much liked by a Santhal. They are regarded sacred by the members of the *Baske* clan only. The *Murmus* perform a household ritual by sacrificing a sheep. Pigeons make their homes in Santhal families. They are kept for food and sacrifice. The Santhals believe that the pigeons are peace-loving birds and do not make their nests in quarrelsome families. Cocks are specially reared for fights. The Santhal men enjoy cock fight which takes place between villages or between clans. It brings laurels and prestige to the winning team. Parrots are sometimes kept in confinement. So, it is seen that the Santhals keep animals for monetary gain as also for pleasure.

The animals are inherited from the father to the son. Unmarried sons get double the share of the livestock, one to meet the marriage expenses. Married daughters get no share but, unmarried ones get a calf as they have to give to the brother of the groom. The livestock that is owned by a daughter-in-law (those that she receives from her father, brother or husband) is not divided. She is free to give it to anyone she likes or may pass it over to her unmarried sons after her death.

## Animals in Medicine

In the field of medicine also, man got his preliminary knolwedge from the animals. Bodding (1927) reports that the Santhals have watched the lizard and the mongoose closely to see what they do for the sting of scorpions and for snakebite. The plants which they ate or rubbed themselves against were used by man and found effective. Bodding (1927) also points out that the Santhals learnt the medicine of cobra bite from old 'Hanuman' — the Monkey - God of Hindus who was treating and curing the young ones, bitten by a cobra. Apart from learning the art of curing from the animals, the Santhals use extracts or parts of the animals as amulets or medicines. Some of the medicines used by the Santhals of Midnapore (now Medinipur) district are given here.

For headaches, blood of a garden lizard is smeared on the forehead. Fat of iguana is applied on the sores of a cow caused during ploughing. Toad's fat is applied on the head to cure head sores. Snail's oil is used for ear sore. Pig's fat is massaged on the body to relieve, muscular as well as arthritic pains. For swollen body in the case of beri-beri, porcupine excreta mixed with coconut oil is massaged all over the body. Eggs of humming birds are eaten for atrophy in babies. Bear's fur tied around the neck as amulet cures high fever. There are also other medicines prepared from sparrows, doves, deers, peacocks, etc. Sometimes claws of tiger or bear are tied around children with a belief that they would become brave and strong as these animals. Further, the Santhals have their own methods of preparing medicines from animal sources.

## Animals in Art and Folklore

The Santhals have utilized figures of human beings, animals, birds and trees, hunting and dancing scenes as well as geometric figures to ornament their walls. Among the animals, elephants with riders, horses, tigers, cows, deers, fowls, ducks, crows and pigeons, also fish, scorpions and snakes or hooded cobra, butterflies are depicted on the walls. By this a sense of security and serenity is felt. Some of the paintings are associated with rituals while others are done purely for decorative purposes. The customs and beliefs leave an impact on the paintings specific to different clan groups. Sometimes, the Santhals believe that these wall paintings or *patua* paintings will drive away the evil forces.

"Tribal lore embodies the ancient observations and customs, the notions, beliefs, traditions, value systems and moral laws of a community, or a tribe" (Daniel, 1991 : 121). Santhal folklore is varied and colourful and centres around plants and animals and human beings. The animal world specially finds a prominent place in the folklore of the Santhals (Bodding, 1990; Bompas, 1991). Tiger, jackal, leopard, pigs, fowl, crab, etc. feature in many stories. Some of them speak of monkeys, bears, etc., bringing up human children or giving birth to human children and human mothers giving birth to animals. Thus we find a close interrelationship between humans and animals. These tales do not differentiate the world of man from that of animals.

The animal world plays multiple roles in Santhal life. It has to be noted that the wild animals usually retain their Santhali names and the domesticated ones are often distinguished by local or English words. This throws some light on their acquiantance with wild animals prior to the domesticated ones.

## REFERENCES

Biswas, P. C., 1956, *Santals of Santal Parganas,* New Delhi : Bharatiya Adimjati Sevak Sangh.

Bodding, P. O., 1927, 'Santal Medicine : Studies in Santal Medicine and Connected Folklore', *Memoirs of the Asiatic Society of Bengal,* 10, (2). Calcutta.

____________, 1990, *Santal Folk Tales,* Volume I, II, III. New Delhi : Gian Publishing House.

Bompas, C. H., 1981, *Folklore of the Santal Parganas,* New Delhi : Ajay Book Service.

Daniel, S. C., 1991, 'Understanding tribal lore by means of intention theory of meaning' in B. N. Saraswati (Ed.), *Tribal Thought and Culture,* pp. 121-127.

New Delhi : Concept.

Pfeffer, Georg, 1984, 'Santhal Totemism', *South Asian Anthropologist* 5(1) : 37-43.

Saraswati, B. N., 1991, 'Tribal Cosmogony : Primal vision of man and cosmos' in B. N. Saraswati (Ed.), *Tribal Thought and Culture,* pp. 63-79. New Delhi : Concept.

# 4

# TRIBAL LIFE IN ASSOCIATION WITH ANIMALS

*Ajit Kumar Aditya* and *Prasanta Chatterjee*

The traditional dwelling place of the Santhals and other tribal groups is considered to be the Santhal Parganas in the Chota Nagpur plateau in Bihar. They are also widely distributed in the states of Bihar, Orissa, West Bengal and Tripura. They inhabit the hilly areas in close association with many wild animals. In fact, animals cannot be removed from their lifestyle. Due to the growth of human population, civilization and deforestation, they have been forced to migrate from their traditional dwelling places in the hilly and forest areas to the different parts of the country (Sachchidananda, 1965). This has not, however, affected their relationship with the animals. The association between tribal life and animal is very strong because they have lived together from the ancient times. While some of the animals considered as very useful were kept in close contact with the people, the less useful ones were not kept in the houses. They have understood the utility of the animals and accordingly some of them have become pet and others not. The active animals were quickly brought under their control and made pet. Utility of inactive or less active animals was also understood by them. These animals were not made pets but remained in association with the people.

**Man and Animals**

A story of the Santhals tells about God Shiva and Goddess Durga not only giving origin to man but also animals in their surroundings and in the Universe. Others believe that *Maran Buru*, the Supreme authority, was responsible for the origin to the animals. In the living world, plants originated earlier than the animals and by way of a complicated and complex process of evolution, animals have evolved into the highest intelligent creatures, the human beings. It also reveals that man has originated next to birds and both of them have a common origin from reptiles. The Santhal's knowledge about the origin of animals on the earth is in line with the present-day scientific opinion.

**Clans and the Totems**

The *Pilcu Haram* and *Pilcu Budhi* are the first man and woman respectively. They believe that the two of them were the first progenitors of the Santhal clans. The clans — *Hansdak, Ayang Soren* and *Pauria* — have emerged from three different animals : duck, cobra and pigeon, respectively, and these animals are totems in their societies (Ferreira, 1922). *Hansdak* has evolved from duck (*gede*) which is its totem. They never eat that animal. *Ayang* means the snake cobra. There is a strong belief among the Santhals that the *Ayang Soren* clan has originated from the cobra snake itself. Whenever, the members of this clan see a cobra, they smear vermilion as part of worshiping it to win its grace. The clan *Pauria* is believed to owe origin to the pigeon (*paura*). A myth bespeaks of a serious disturbance in peaceful relations between different Santhal clans. At that time a few members of their community thought about the peace of the Santhal soc and worshipped the pigeon since they were of the opinion tha this bird is the symbol of peace. With the grace of that ancestral Pigeon God, peace was restored in the Santhal society. Later, the honest and saintly people got the title 'Pauria'. They were the founders of the *Pauria* clan.

The clan names *Murmu, Kisku, Hembram, Marndi, Soren,*

*Tudu, Baske, Pauria, Chore* and *Bedea,* etc., are derived from the names of their totems. The totems are not restricted to the animals only but the plants may also be the totems for some clans. The clans have evolved from plant and animal creatures that are worshipped as their totems : *Hansdak* (wild goose), *Marndi* (Grass), *Soren* (constellation pleiades), *Besra* (hawk), *Pauria* (pigeon), *Chore* (lizard), and *Bedea* (sheep). A person must not kill or hurt or destroy his totemic animal or plant. He may not marry a member of the same totemic division. A woman always adopts the clan of her husband after marriage and comes back to her paternal clan whenever she is divorced or widowed. The members of the other clans avoid marriage with the members of two clans, *Besra* and *Chore* who are considered to be of lower status and inferior to other clans. Marriage is admissible within a clan and with different sub-clans of a clan. The incidence of incest between members of a sub-clan is a much more serious offence.

## Organisms and their Control

The Santhals consider man as Supreme not only for his ability to speak but also for his higher intelligence and mental development in comparison with animals. It is for this reason that the animals are always controlled by human beings. Further, longevity of man exceeds that of animals. Some Santhals also say that the longevity of a few animals (fowl, duck, rabbit, goat, etc.) is under the control of man because they can be killed and consumed whenever they wish.

One *Tudu* family in a village may not rear or touch a pig and not take pork. Another *Tudu* family in the same village, however, may rear and touch the pig (*sukri*) and consume pork. Their taboo systems also vary from one clan to the other. Santhals cannot eat beaf. They respect cows as God who is responsible for the betterment of their family and the society at large.

The festival cf *Sohrae* takes place in the month of January mainly to worship pet cows in an open ground near the villages (Mukherjee, 1959). The Committee determines the appropriate place in the ground for the sacrifice. The priest *Naeke* draws a structure with the dust of the sunned rice *Atoua Chaule*. There are separate rectangles for 13 gods and goddesses. They render worship to these compartments separately. Though the process of offering of the chicken (*Sim hopan*) is not always the same in every Santhal village, it is mandatory to offer the blood of the animal. The Santhal priest offers the blood from different chickens in the 13 rectangular compartments in the same way. It is necessary to indicate that out of the 14 sacrificed chickens only three chickens' bodies are kept aside for the priest (*Naeke*), first leader (*Manjhi*), and the second leader (*Peranik*). The hotchpotch (*leto*) with chicken meat (*gill*) is taken by all the male villagers while three council members (*Naeke*, *Manjhi*, *Haramand Peranik*) make a special hotchpotch with the meat of chicken and the dust of sunned rice for them in a pot of leaves of Sal tree and eat it. There is a restriction among the Santhals that no female will go to the spot of the *Sohrae* and take the sacred hotchpotch.

The Santhals use animals for various purposes such as religious, medicinal, economic, cultivation, hunting and as consumable items, etc. which also forms the bases for classifying them. Today some tribals are engaged in buying and selling the cow, goat, pig, sheep, buffalo, duck and fowl to meet their financial needs. They use bulls, oxen and buffaloes for cultivation. Moreover, the tribals get milk from cows which is a nutritious food for the children and adults. Some of them sell it too. Their body requirements of protein are met from pig, goat, sheep and fowl meat.

Some undomesticated animals such as birds, reptiles and fishes help in their economy also. In the rainy season when the ponds, ditches and canals get flooded, the tribals collect a large number of fishes. They use them as food material and sell off the excess to earn money. In the tribal society, collecting, depositing and selling of the excretory products of pet animals is common. These products provide good composite fertilizer which is cheap. They store it and scatter it as the manure in the field before cultivation. They also use the dry cowdung as fuel.

## Animals in Medicine

The tribals have inherited their beliefs from the ancestors. Though on account of modernization they have started using the modern medicines, many of them still rely on the indigenous medicines handed down by their ancestors and which are prepared by themselves or by the *Ojha* (medicine man). The medicines produced from animal bodies or from their products are quite effective and have been found to be beneficial, even better than many modern medicines. Some examples are :

(a) The tribals use an oil produced from the fat deposits of *Varanus* — a reptile for treating burning ulcers and some kind of bone ache.

(b) The accessory respiratory organ of scaleless fish such as *Kai/Magur/Singhi* is made into a paste which is applied on the head of abnormal persons. Like the above, a number of animals are used as medicines in the society.

(c) If the Jeol group of fishes (*Singhi/Magur*) strikes any person with its poisonous spine, the tribals prepare a paste from a small piece of the small intestine of the striker fish and apply it to the affected area and they believe it gives relief from pain.

(d) Patients suffering from cardiac problems and asthma are treated with a soup of small frog and respiratory gills of the *Magur* fish, respectively.

(e) If the heart of *Mabuia* — a reptile is placed in the mouth of a patient who is about to die, he would recover.

(f) The milk of sheep is used as medicine for tongue ulcers.

(g) Cow's urine and mud are used as medicine for boils and ulcers.

(h) The outer coat of a crocodile is used as medicine for the *Kala Doba*.

(i) If the barbed *Singhi* fish hurts with its poisonous spine on their bodies, Santhals use the smoke of dry cow-dung as medicine.

(j) The *Magur* fish has a great medicinal value. The medicine is prepared with *Magur* fish and mustard oil and from some medicinal plants. The living *Magur* fish is put into boiling mustard oil along with some medicinal plants. They believe that if this fish moves freely within the boiling oil in a live condition pure medicine will be prepared for that patient. They also believe that so long as the fish remains alive, the medicinal value of the oil will persist.

**Animals as Food**

The tribals usually go in a group for hunting. The pet dog becomes their guide. The bird titlark is very useful to them to catch the others with the help of a trap. They train a titlark to make a sound on a particular signal. This bird is then put in a cage attached with the trap. They wait with the cage by the side of a river and at an appropriate moment let out a signal. When the titlark cries out, other birds in the vicinity rush to help and eventually get trapped. The eggs of all birds are collected by them. Sometimes, they kill rabbits in the jungle and host a feast in the evening in which most of the villagers participate.

They also train the mongoose and keep it as pet. The mongoose is the worst enemy of snakes. The tribals take the flesh of the snakes excluding the mouth and head portion because they know that the poison glands and the bony and muscular part of the biting apparatus are lodged in the mouth and the head. This shows that the anatomy of the snake is known to them.

Santhals also have a good deal of knowledge about the anatomy and physiology of chicken and fowl. They take out the feathers and skin and dress the fowl, but before cutting it into pieces the animal is washed and dissected. The crop and the sac containing the undigested foodgrains are kept aside. The gizzard — the muscular cushion along with half-ground material and the intestines are discarded since they may contain some infective bacteria and viruses which may cause infection. They also remove the eyes from the head since some material that would be harmful to humans may be present here.

The tribals believe that any object in nature is creation of and gift from the God. Sometimes they offer prayer to the animal itself directly. On the day of the *Sohrae* or *Bandna* festival they worship cows with vermilion (*sindur*), mustard oil, paddy and *Durba* grass. They believe that on the day of *Bandna* before the sunset if a cow breaks the sacred egg of hen, it brings good luck to the owner of the cow.

## Concluding Remarks

The Santhals have a distinctive tradition of art : song, painting, drama, dance and folk tales. The songs and dances expressing their traditional art are based on the habits of animals. They also compose songs depicting the nature of the animals. Sometimes one or two persons dance with an artificial animal accompanied by a group of singers. The dancer who dances with an ornamented effigy of a horse looks like a rider on a horse. They have this type of dance usually during festivals. They sometimes keep the painting of certain animals by the side of the door.

The medicine man (*Ojha*) enjoys a respectable position. He has a vast experience of the use of animal bodies for various medicinal purposes. He can prepare very useful medicines from the animal tissues. Though the traditional beliefs, prejudices (about the rituals, medicines, cooking, music, art, painting, etc.) are still seen being practised by the Santhals, few are attracted by the modernization of the world, and try to imitate the modern works of art. Their modern generation has not remained confined to old beliefs and ideas. They have been influenced by the modernization at every level. Thus their own traditional arts and culture now reflect the modern world.

REFERENCES

Archer, W.G., 1945, "The Forcible Marriage", in *Man in India.*

____________, 1947, "Ritual Friendship in Santhal Society", in *Man in India.*

Bhowmik, K.L., 1986, *Tribal India, a profile in India Ethology,* Calcutta.

Bedding, P. O., 1990, *Santal Folk Tales* (in three vols.) New Delhi.

Dutta Majumdar, N., *1956, The Santhal - A Study in Culture-Change,* Calcutta.

Ferreria, J. V., 1992, *Totemism in India,* London.

Mukherjee, C., 1922, *The Santhal,* Calcutta.

Sachchidananda, 1965, *Profiles of Tribal Culture in Bihar,* Calcutta.

# 5

# SANTHAL CONCEPT OF FOOD

*Indrani Bhattacharyya (Chakraborty)*

---

In the present paper an attempt has been made to study how the Santhal define and classify food, perceive its function in the human body, think of time and space with regard to cooking, perceive taste and flavour of food and relate food to emotions and behaviour. This study was conducted in a Santhal village, Patherghata, of Bolpur - Sriniketan Block, Birbhum, West Bengal, located at around 16 km. to the north-east of Bolpur Police Station.

The Santhal term for food is *jom nu* which means any solid, liquid or gaseous substance which strengthens the body. They say, *Dare lage jom, Jivi banca lage jom, Jivi tehen lage jom* to mean that food is required to provide energy, to save one's life and above all to perform daily activities. They have a clear idea that food provides energy. This energy keeps them active as a result of which they are able to perform daily activities and enjoy life.

## Two Categories

The Santhals classify *jom nu* into two main categories : *jom,* i.e. solid, chewable food, and *nu,* i.e. drinkable and smoky items. All food items grouped under these two broad categories show that the gastronomic range of the Santhal is very wide and cover not only corns of grasses but also large quadruped animals. These two categories of food are further classified according to, (a) the method of cooking, (b) ingredients used, (c) time of consumption, and (d) physical state (i.e. hot,stale, etc.)

Santhals not only eat or drink their food items, but also think about their role or function in the body. They say, "We have a body like a machine and we eat food that is the machine oil. Just as oil is necessary to keep a machine active, we also feed our body", and thus perceive food as something which provides efficiency for work. They say that if anyone eats without measure, he gets pain in the stomach, the food is not digested, the stomach rumbles and gets disturbed. Bodding makes a similar observation in his study on Santhal medicine and connected folklore. According to him, the Santhals say, "We have a body like railway engine. We eat food, that is the coal. Just as they feed an engine with coal and water, so we also feed our body. We break wind; that is the smoke that gets out. What we eat, first passes into the belly; there the food is diluted. If there is too little water, we feel thirsty and have to drink. Finally it all turns into the substance of rice-water and this is turned into blood" (Bodding, 1940:5). Thus the Santhals comprehend functions of food in the human body in their own way.

**Ingredients of Food**

It is observed that the nature of food consumed is in opposition to the climate. Wet food is eaten in dry season and dry food in wet season. On summer days they cook and eat mainly cold, stale rice with gruel, boiled curries, etc, which, they believe keeps the body cool. The meal eaten in the fields also consists of stale rice mixed with water. During winter and rainy seasons they eat warm, freshly boiled rice, without gruel. Other foods cooked in the wet season are cereal, meat, fish, vegetables, etc., which have been dried in the sun by them in the previous summer. Thus the Santhal's mode of cooking and use of ingredients are governed by the season.

Cooking not only in day-tò-day life, but different festivals is also regulated by time. For example, a *Naeke* (the village priest) cannot cook first fruits of *Matkom* (the *Mahua*), and *Sarjom* (the

Sal) , new leaves and the winter rice crop, before offering them to the spirits at *Baha* (the flower festival) and *Janthar* (the harvest festival). The male members, who want to eat the head of any sacrificial offering, cannot cook or eat any non-vegetarian item in their own houses in the evening prior to sacrifice. The wife of *Dihri* (the hunting superintendent ) is forbidden to cook any non-vegetarian item until her husband returns from the jungle. These regulations are meant to demonstrate people's respect to the spirits. Cooking of *piṭhạ* (sweet or salted cake), a food of religious and social importance is also regulated by time. *Arsa piṭhạ,* for example, is prepared to welcome the guest at any social ceremony; *buka piṭhạ* is made only on the occasion of name-giving ceremony of a new-born baby; *dombok piṭhạ* is prepared during festivals in the months of November-December; *jel piṭhạ* must be prepared at *Sohrae* (the harvest festival) and so on. Not only *piṭhạ*, but cooking of some other foods such as *nim-dik-mandi, nimsure*,etc., is also regulated by time. *Nim-dak-mandi* (rice-gruel with margosa leaves) must be cooked and eaten at the time of name-giving ceremony of a new-born baby to remove pollution of the spirits and the whole village. *Nim sure* (rice and *Margosa* leaves mixed) must be cooked and eaten by all the members of a household when the farmer comes home after having sown the first paddy to ensure that the flies will not eat the ears of the corn.

## Regulated Cooking

Cooking is not only regulated by time, but also by space. Cooking of certain food items must be done at defined spaces. Meat of animals sacrified to *Abge bonga* (sub-clan spirit) for example, must be cooked and eaten within the flour circle made by the officiating person where sacrifice has been performed. All the left-overs are burnt. The Santhals believe that if they come with the sacrificial meat in the village, the spirit will enter the village along with it and may bring harm to other sub-clans. Flesh of any animal sacrified at the *jaherthan* (the sacred grove ) must be cooked and eaten there itself. This belief is the same as that associated with the *Abge bonga.*

Remains of sacrifies to the *Bahre bonga* (village outskirts spirit) must be cooked and eaten outside the village lest the spirit will be angry and cause harm to the whole village. Even if the meat of oxen or cows is brought in the village, it is not taken inside the house. It must be cooked and eaten in the courtyard. They don't take the vessels in which the cow's or ox's meat has been cooked inside the house. It is strictly forbidden for any Santhal to cook or eat anything at the *kharai* (the threshing ground). It is believed that if the prohibition is not followed, the *Kharaichatani bonga* (the spirit of the threshing ground) will become very angry. These examples reveal that the Santhal cooking is regulated by space on the one hand, and by their belief in the spirit world, on the other.

The Santhals are also not indifferent to good or bad taste of food. They actually divide their 'food world' into two categories, (1) *arak sakam jom nu* which includes all common edible items such as vegetables, cereals, roots, tubers,etc. and, (2) *bhạgi bhạgi jom nu* which includes all tasty items such as *jelhako* (meat and fish), *toạdạhi* (milk and curd), *gurgotạm* (molasses and clarified butter), *hạnḍi* (rice-beer) , etc.

They have a common term, *sibil* for tasty items and *saba* for tasteless foods. A food which they find tasteless is struck off from the list of their edible items as the crow, dog and few others. They say that the meat of these animals and birds is not tasty. So they don't eat it . Generally the Santhals consider *bulun* (salt) as an essential item to make any curry savoury. They often say, *"Dharte re-culunge sibil horte sibil"* which means salt and talk — these two things are tasteful in this world. They have a saying : what pleases the mouth is salt; what pleases the eyes is turmeric; what pleases the nose are spices; what pleases the lips is pepper and when you combine all these things, the result is most agreeable (Bodding, 1940 :456 ) . If any of these items is not added in proper proportion to a preparation, then it is *saba*, i.e. tasteless. Generally Santhals consider meat of pig and rice-beer as the most tasteful food in the world. They greet and honour their guests with these two items. They say that the food prepared by *lat* (roasting by wrapping in leaves) and *rapak'* (roasting on embers) processes is savoury, though no spices are used in either of them. The Santhals have a common term, *sạ* for flavour. They have also the idea of bad and good flavour. They don't eat any food which has *risgi sạ* (bad flavour) but eat happily food having *mạjiạ sạ* (good flavour). For example, they don't eat mole, jackal, etc., for their *risgi sạ,* i.e. bad flavour. On the other hand, the peculiar acid-sweet flavour of rice-beer is a favourite with them. Thus they classify items of their food according to flavour,i.e. food items with good flavour and food items with bad flavour.

## Most Sacred Drink

*Hạnḍi,* i.e. ricebeer, is the most sacred and indispensable drink of the Santhals. According to a myth, the Supreme deity, *Maran Buru,* taught the first human pair of *Pilcu Haram* and *Pilcu Budhi* to prepare *hạnḍi.* It is, therefore, a very sacred food to them. The festivals of the Santhals would appear lifeless without ricebeer. It may be noted that the Santhals drink not only to enjoy its taste, but to become nearly intoxicated, so as to forget the troubles of this world. Bodding (1940 : 496) also made a similar observation: according to what has been told, they pass through all the stages, some become hilarious, others melancholy, some become abusive, others sing and tell stories; some become vile, lascivious and pugnacious, others moral, amiable and so on. The avowed objective is to be able to forget for a few hours the miseries of this world and feel like kings, as they put it.

*Hạnḍi* is also regarded as purificatory. The religious and communal pollutions incurred at each critical juncture of life, i.e. at birth, initiation, marriage and death, are removed by the libation of ricebeer to the spirits and then drinking of it by the whole village. Not only at the turning points of their lifecycle, but also pollution on certain other occasions is removed by drinking of ricebeer. At *Sohrae* for example, when the code of sexual conduct is deliberately relaxed and men and women indulge in debauchery and drunkenness, they consider themselves polluted and purify themselves by drinking *chatiar hạnḍi* (beer for cleansing onself socially) served by the *Jog-Manjhi* (the guardian of village morals).

Ricebeer is also considered a food which symbolizes greeting. A Santhal man or woman at any social gathering or at any meeting or at any ceremony is greeted with a drink of ricebeer. Thus, ricebeer is not only a most important drink item for the Santhals, but also regulates their behaviour with other persons.

*Gurtaben khạjạri* (molasses, flattened rice and parched rice) is another important food to the Santhals. It is called *sandes*. A boy when going to his sister's father-in-law's house must take with him some *sandes* (*gurtaben khạjạri*) to show honour to his sister-in-law.

To guard against the evil eye, some Santhal women take a little of the food that is to be made into curry in their hand and holding it over the vessel used, they say, "May it have a spell cast on it, may it get teeth." The meaning is that if any woman with an evil eye has looked on, no spell may be cast on food. It may be eaten and digested without any stomach-ache, vomiting or diarrhoea. They also use some food to guard themselves against a witch. The eating of *guạ gandhari aṛak* (leaves of *Amaranthus gangeticus*) for instance guards them against the evil eye of a witch.

From the foregoing discussion it is evident that the Santhals, whose food world has a very vast range, classify it using multiple criteria. They think of food as a fuel which keeps active the machinery arrangements of the body. Time and space are two important criteria which regulate their cooking and also eating. They enjoy the taste and flavour of their food items. Their emotions and behaviour are regulated by food.

## REFERENCE

Bodding, P. O., 1940, How the Santals live, Studies in Santal Medicine and connected Folklore, p-III, *Memoirs of the Royal Asiatic Society of Bengal*, Vol-X, No. 3. Calcutta.

# 6

# SOUNDS FROM A SANTHAL VILLAGE

*Peter Pannke*

---

In November, 1994, a Swiss sound artist, a German composer and musicologist, Peter Pannke, accompanied by Dr. Onkar Prasad, an anthropologist of Visva-Bharati at Santiniketan, visited the villages of Bandlodanga, Kolapukurdanga, Mohisadel, Pathorghata and Baganpara, all located in the neighbourhood of Santiniketan in the Birbhum district of West Bengal as part of a research project devoted to the Santhals undertaken by the Indira Gandhi National Centre for the Arts in New Delhi under the direction of Prof. Baidyanath Saraswati. As the purpose was to study the Santhal conception of sound, we recorded not only music but also as much of the daily activities of these villages as we could during the week we had at our disposal. The result of this visit was presented on a Compact Disc (CD) under the title "Honeywind - Sounds From A Santal Village."* Following is the information given in the booklet of the CD.

The Santhals live in the north-eastern part of India. Numbering about four million people, they constitute the second

---

* Available as Wergo CD SM 1612-2 at Schott Wergo Music Media GmbH, Weihergarten 5, 55116 Mainz, Germany.

largest tribal community of India. They are of proto-australoid origin and speak Santhali, a sub-family of the austro-asiatic group of languages. Antedating both Aryans and Dravidians, they belong to the *adivasis* — a term used for the various tribes which lived in India before. Although the ecology has changed considerably, the Santhals still inhabit the partially forested areas of the provinces of Bengal, Bihar and Orissa. Their belief in *bongas,* nature-spirits, sets them apart from their neighbours, and they have always strictly refrained from mixing with the surrounding population. When the East India Company threatened to bereave them of their ancient territories in the middle of the 19th century, 30,000 Santhals, armed with spears, marched towards Calcutta to protest. Although the rebellion was crushed, the government later granted them their own district called 'Santhal Pargana', and, to a certain extent, their own governance. Due to economic difficulties in the 20th century, many Santhals took up work in the coal mines of Chota Nagpur, but the majority still live in their own villages, with agriculture as their main source of livelihood.

Although the villages where the recordings were made are located near the town of Santiniketan and are, at least partly, touched by modern life, they are surrounded by trees, and the *jaher,* the sacred grove which is maintained in every village, reminds the Santhals of their close association with the forest. It is the village street, however, that dominates the scene—not only as a thoroughfare where bullockcarts, bicycles, scooters and an occasional bus move, but there is also a dance floor, a council chamber and a court of justice. Although there are differences in the economic status, the Santhals have a remarkable sense of democratic equality.

The mud walls of the houses are softly curved and reflect light and sound in a very indirect way. Thatched roofs cover them gently. While sounds from outside appear a bit muffled here, they are not completely shut out. All the inhabitants are in constant contact with their acoustic environment, which is a significant factor of their life. The rooms center around an open courtyard. Most of them have a verandah where people sit and work or chat. Ricebeer is a necessary ingredient of any festival which is held here. There may be a pigstall and a vegetable garden. Behind the trees the open fields begin from where the constant buzz of crickets comes in. Flutes are played by the boys and girls who herd the cattle to their grazing ground. The place where people gather in the evening is a bit removed from the village.

The Santhals have their own and very original conception of sound. They consider their acoustic environment as consisting of three categories : *sade,* produced by striking together different objects; *rak,* which is made up of the calls of animals; and *aran,* human sounds which are again subdivided into *ror* (speech) and *rar* (song). Sounds are always an important indicator of anything going on inside or outside the village, a means of ritual and practical orientation in time and space. Certain sounds are attributed with auspiciousness or inauspiciousneses; if, for example, a jackal is heard from the place where a certain *bonga* is worshipped, it is considered as an indication of an evil spirit entering the village, and so is the barking of a dog from the eastern side. When a vulture cries hovering over the village, a disease may approach. There are many different names for the crows of a cock according to the times they occur; if it is heard between the evening meal and midnight, this is considered as an evil omen as well, and the cock will be killed or sold the next morning. On the other hand, certain sounds indicate good omens as the coming of the rains. The voices of humans, animals and nature blend into a harmonious, constantly moving stream of sound. The total absence of it, however, is an indication of danger of some kind. If a village is considered polluted by a birth or a death or by an epidemic, any playing or singing is prohibited before it is purified, and any ritual music is always preceded by worship of the spirits.

## The Instruments

*Tirio,* the instrument most favoured by the Santhals, is a bamboo flute with seven holes. It is viewed as a symbol of love and seduction.

*Dhodro banàm* is a bowed instrument carved out of a single log of wood of a tree which, according to a Santhal story, grew out of the flesh of a human being. It consists of a belly *(lac)* covered with an animal skin on which rests the bridge *(sadom,* lit. horse), an open chest (*koram*), a short neck *(hotok)* and a head *(bohok)* which is often beautifully carved in the shape of a human head, a couple or even a whole group of humans, or of animals. If the shape is a head, the tuning peg is inserted in the ear *(lutur),* and the gut string comes out of the mouth.

*Phet banam* is a fretless stringed instrument with three or four strings. The 'waisted belly' is completely covered by animal skin.

*Tumdak,* otherwise known as *madol,* is a two-faced drum with a body of burnt clay. Both heads — the left one broader than the right — are covered by bullock hide and are beaten by the left and right hand.

*Tamak* is a bowl-shaped kettle drum. Its body is made of thin metal sheets, covered by bullock hide and beaten by a pair of sticks.

*Jhunko* is an onomatopoeic description of the sound of the ankle bells, which are cast in metal in the shape of buds and tied to the feet of the dancers from where they produce rhythmical sounds.

*Singa* is an S-shaped wind instrument played in pairs in weddings. Made of brass or copper, it is usually constructed in three pieces with a mouthpiece at the blowing end and a conic opening at the other.

## The Recordings

The recordings on the CD are arranged in the form of a soundwalk through a Santhal village, lasting from early morning until night. Singing and dancing as social activities, however, occur only in the evening, while individual songs are also sung during work in the fields, or in the forest. Some of these songs are instrumental pieces set into the context of the walk through the village, until finally in the evening the place of the festival is reached. The dance songs are heard in the sequence in which they actually occurred.

### 1. APPROACHING A VILLAGE IN THE EARLY MORNING

When approaching a Santhal village in the early morning, the first impression is not that of a village but of a small forest. Crickets provide a constant drone to the acoustic environment. A train passing by is an indication that the outside world is not far. We pass trees populated by a multitude of chirping birds, and encounter a few goats and dogs when we enter the main street. The crows of cocks announce the wake of the day, while the ducks are busy in a little pond.

## 2. SOHRAE MELODY PLAYED ON THE TIRIO

The *Sohrae* melody which is played here on the *tirio* belongs to a festival celebrated after the harvest in December or January in honour of the unmarried elder daughter of the first Santhal couple. Lasting for five days, all social restrictions on sexual behaviour are withdrawn deliberately by the village authorities to give the village boys and girls a sense of freedom. The *Sohrae* dance is usually danced in the village street. The girls stand in a straight line from one end of the street to the other, and the village boys, including children and elder males, stand in front of them. *Sohrae* songs are also sung when the earth has become barren after the harvest, as a symbolic attempt to restore fertility of the earth.

## 3. VILLAGE WAKING UP

Women's voices announce that the village is waking up. The morning train is passing by. Although the rails are about 1 km. away, the sharp sound runs through the gentle village life.

## 4. DON SONG ACCOMPANIED BY PHET BANAM, JHUNKO AND TAMAK

This *don* song was recorded in the courtyard of Bazar Hembrom, who is not only a performer and singer, but also a skilled instrument maker. He plays the *phet banam,* while other members of the family accompany *jhunko* and *tumdak. Don* songs, which often have a jocular content, are sung and danced during the marriage time by both boys and girls. The *mandawa* mentioned here is the strawshed erected on five bamboo poles for the marriage ceremony. Following is a *don* song :

*Mandawa lataree*
*Chameda latarre*
*Tokoe nader keda*
*Gunda busup*
*Nowa gunda busup*
*Lebet teget kolsa tegen*
*Hidgi digir*
*Hariar ge dhubi ghasin*
*Janam nacoy goy*
*Janam nacoy*

[Under the shed thatched for the marriage ceremony,
Who brought the straw and its pieces?
The straw and its pieces turn to dust
Because of the dancing on it.
There grew the green grass.]

5. AT THE VILLAGE POND

Passing the village pond we hear the cackle of ducks and crows of cocks, while the women talk and wash their utensils. A bullock cart crosses the road, followed by a family of ducks and a scooter.

6. DON SONG ACCOMPANIED BY PHET BANAM, JHUNKO AND TAMAK

Bazar Hembrom is singing here in a mixture of Bengali and Santhali, accompanied by *phet banam, jhunko* and *tamak.* The song describes the neglected state of the *manjhithan,* the pedestal constructed for the worship of the predecessors of the village headman called *Manjhi.* Following is a *lagre* song :

*Cetan kulhi manjhithan*
*Latar kulhi manjhithan*
*Tala kulhi manjhithan*
*Jonome tuwar*
*Haere haere kuri kora*
*Oto hisaliya re*
*Tala kulhi manjhithan*
*Jonome tuwar*

[There is a *manjhithan* on the upper end of the street.
There is a *manjhithan* on the lower end of the street.
There is a *manjhithan* on the middle part of the street.
But from the very beginning this one is neglected.
It appears that both boys and girls are jealous of it.
There is a *manjhithan* in the middle part of the street.
But from the very beginning it is neglected.]

## 7. WALKING AROUND THE VILLAGE

We pass from the main street into a side lane. Children are playing here, and we get glimpses into the courtyards where people are busy husking grain in a mortar. A child is playing with a transistor radio broadcasting popular music.

## 8. LAGRE MELODY PLAYED ON DHODRO BANAM AND JHUNKO

A *lagre* melody is played here on *dhodro banam* and *jhunko.* Lagre songs are performed during the hot season in order to invoke rain and get relief from the intense heat.

## 9. CHILDREN AND ANIMALS IN THE VILLAGE

A new-born goat is bleating in the street, and children are feeding the cattle with grass. Listening carefully, we hear the sounds of the whole village in the background.

## 10. DON SONG ACCOMPANIED BY PHET BANAM, JHUNKO AND TAMAK

Bazar Hembrom is singing another *don* song accompanied by *phet banam, jhunko* and *tamak.* Following is a *don* song :

*Nowa dhartima dhiri talare*
*Ohae aman rup dai upal bahare*
*Nowa dhartima dhiri talare*
*Ohae aman rup dai sagen sakamre*
*Hasa renan tumdak*
*Dimi tinak dinem payra eneca*
*Notem kojok anre*
*Hana din upi leka*
*In tayomte*
*Phagun bonga beha acur lenge*
*Cere cupri ko udau lenge*
*Nowa dharti ma buru talare*
*Ohae aman rup dai upal behare*
*Ohae aman rup dai sagan sakamre*

[In the middle of the stones of this earth,
O sister, your beauty is just like a lotus !
In the middle of the stones of this earth,
O sister, your beauty is just like a new leaf !
The *tumdak* is made of soil,
O daughter, for how many days will you play in knee-deep water ?
Someday you have to come to look after me.
That day you will be after me like the *jhadi* insect.
On the day of the full moon in the month of *phalgun*
The birds will be ready to fly
Like the earth in the middle of the hill.
O sister, your beauty is just like a lotus !
O sister, your beauty is just like a new leaf !]

## 11. AT THE BLACKSMITH/WALKING TO PLACE OF THE EVENING FESTIVAL

From the crossroads we pass a small pigstall and take a turn to the cottage of the blacksmith. Meeting here is an occasion for a little chat, and the villagers help the blacksmith working the bellows. A bicycle passes, and a transistor radio is playing near by. From here we leave the village and walk through the trees to the place where the dancing will take place in the evening. Voices of the people already gathered here greet us.

## 12. DON MELODY PLAYED ON DHODRO BANAM

The player of the *dhodro banam* demonstrates his skill with a *don* melody.

## 13. DASAE MELODY PLAYED ON THE TIRIO

For *dasae* young Santhal boys wander from village to village in September or October to beg corn and to take blessings from elderly women.

## 14. DON SONG ACCOMPANIED BY TIRIO

The *tirio* player continues with the melody of a *don* song which he sings too. Following is a *don* song :

*Chameda latarre*
*Mandawa latarre*
*Okoe papistan nutum kidin*
*Caban papistan nutum kidin*
*More goten baren teko*
*Baysi reko durup akan*
*Cakba papistan tumbutena*

[Under the shed thatched for the marriage ceremony

Who is the naughty person who has taken my name ?
Why has that naughty person taken my name ?
I have five elder brothers,
They are attending the meeting now.
Why is that rough person sitting with a bowed head ?]

15. SINGA AND TAMAK

The blowing of the *singa* and beating of the *tamak* announce that a social gathering will take place.

16. DRUM BEATS ON TUMDAK AND TAMAK

Before the dance begins, the beats of the *tumdak* set the rhythm while the *tamak* echoes adds to it. It is the way in which they are played that decides the rhythm and the style of the dancing.

17. GILWARI DANCE SONG ACCOMPANIED BY TUMDAK, TAMAK, JHUNKO, DHODRO BANAM AND TIRIO

*Gilwari* songs are performed either before a public gathering outside the village, as it is happening here, or at midnight. Accompanied by *tumdak* and *tamak,* the purpose is to protect the place and the performers from the influence of evil spirits. Following is a *gilwari* song :

*Tahareta nana tarna*
*Tahareta nana*
*Tahareta nana tarna na nana ho*
*Ore gilwari adha rate kena gilwari*

[Tahareta nana ... (Refrain)
O *gilwari,* why *gilwari* at midnight ?]

18. DRUM BEATS ON TUMDAK AND TAMAK

The drums announce the different dance rhythms which are to follow.

## 19. DON DANCE SONG ACCOMPANIED BY TUMDAK, TAMAK, JHUNKO, PHET BANAM AND TIRIO

While they hear the drum beats, the women position themselves for the *don* dance song which is usually performed at marriages. The men accompany the women playing and dancing in a separate line behind them, and here a *phet banam* player joins in. Following is a *don* song :

*Tis reco sar baha*
*Setonte mosot akan*
*Dhurire nurakan taral basal*
*Ho dhurire nurakan taral basal*
*Adom do sadomko jom ket*
*Adom do nurakan taral basal*
*Ar ho nurakan tarai basal*

[Since when the flowing flower
has dried up due to the intense heat?
The flowers have been spread here and there on the sand,
yes, the flowers have been spread here and there on the sand.
Some someone has taken by hand,
Some have been eaten by the horse,
Some have been scattered here and there,
Yes, some are lying here and there.]

## 20. KARAM DANCE SONG ACCOMPANIED BY TUMDAK, TAMAK, JHUNKO, DHODRO BANAM AND TIRIO

The following *Karam* dance song is first announced by drum beats as well. The festival to which it belongs has its name from the *Karam* tree. In the beginning the *Karam guru* recites a prayer that deals with the creation of the world. *Hihiri* and *pipiri* mentioned here are the ancestral sites from where the Santhals came to their present land. Following is a *Karam* song :

*Taha reta nahre nana ho*
*Taha reta re na nana ho*
*Taha reta re nana re*
*Eh eh eh*
*Hihiri jonom pipiri jonom*
*Jonom cae campa garre*
*Taha reta re nahare nana ho*
*Taha reta re nahare nan ho*
*Sarakan lili bici*
*Sakamakan ciri biri*
*Dejok me se reugume rugume*

[Tahe reta ... (Refrain)
Take birth in *hihiri,* take birth in *pipiri,*
Take birth in the *cae campa* fort !
Taha reta ... (Refrain)
The flowers are swaying beautifully
The leaves are very high.
Climb up the tree slowly !

21. END OF THE FESTIVAL WITH TUMDAK AND TAMAK BEATS

After the festival closes with the last beats of *tumdak* and *tamak,* the forest is still reasonating with crickets and calls of night birds.

---

Acknowledgement : The song texts used in this paper have been translated by Onkar Prasad

# 7

# SANTHAL APPROACH TO SOUNDS

*Onkar Prasad*

Among the Santhal*, a common term for sound is *Saḍe*. Various types of sounds produced by different objects that constitute their soundscape are classified by them mainly under three categories — *Saḍe*, *Aṛaṅ* and *Raḱ*.

The term *Saḍe* is used to refer to sounds produced by different objects as a result of a stroke or collision or friction. Sounds included under this category are those of man, animals and insects other than their calls and those of material objects, e.g. *hoe saḍe* (whizzing of the air), *daḱ saḍe* (sound of water), *rimil saḍe* (roaring of the cloud), *ṭamaḱ saḍe* (sound of the kettle drum), etc.

The term *Aṛaṅ* is used to refer to the purely human voice,e.g. *tala nindere hoṛ aṛaṅ anjomkate setako raḱ keda* (having heard the voice of man, the dog started barking). The rhythmic as well as tonal sounds produced by different musical instruments are also referred to as *aṛaṅ*, e.g. *tumdaḱ bhagi baṅ aṛanoḱ kana* (the *tumdaḱ* is not sounding well).

*Aṛaṅ* is further divided into two sub-categories—*roṛ* (speech sound), e.g. *hoṛko roṛeda* (men are speaking) and *raṛ* (melodic

---

* The Santhals are a tribe of Proto-australoid origin speaking the language of the Mundari group. They, in majority, inhabit the States of Bihar, West Bengal and Orissa. Agriculture is the main source of their livelihood.

sound), e.g. *Baha rar̥* (*Baha* melody), *Sohrae rar̥* (*Sohrae* melody) etc. But, according to the Santhal , there is no sharp distinction between the two, i.e. *ror̥* and *r̥ar̥*. There is a famous aphorism among them—*ror̥ak' tege r̥ar̥ak'* (melody is the prolongation of the ordinary speech).

The term *rak'* is used to refer to the sounds produced by different animals and birds and insects, e.g *setako rak' keda* (the dogs are barking), *cerceṭeće rak' keda* (the house lizard is calling), *sime rak' keda* (the cock is calling),etc. Sounds produced by man when experiencing pain are also termed *rak'* e.g. *kirir kirir* (sound of crying loudly), *kusuk' kusuk'* (sound of sobbing ), etc.

The Santhal divide some sounds of their acoustic enviornment into two categories — *bugi* (auspicious) and *b̥aric'* (inauspicious). For example, when the bird, *sasan cẽr̥ẽ* (the golden oriole) calls out *pio pio* sitting on a tree near a Santhal house, it indicates the coming of a guest to that house. Here a Santhal would say, *"Pio cẽr̥ẽye rak' keda, okoe per̥a coe hijuk'"* (the golden oriole is crying, some guest will come). When the same bird calls out *kher kher* it is supposed to bring death news of a dear relative.

The cock generally makes three calls after midnight and before the rising of the sun. But, if it makes an untimely call between *kedok daka jom* (evening meal) and *tala ńinde* (midnight),it is considered inauspicious. The Santhal believe that it is an indication of an evil spirit entering the house of its owner which may cause some harm to any member of the household. In order to ward off the spirit, the villagers trace the house , kill the cock, and eat it the next morning. Sometimes the cock is also sold.

The call of *toyo* (the jackal) from the direction of the place where *Jatra bonga* ( a powerful spirit) is worshipped is believed to cause an evil spirit to enter the village. Generally, a jackal makes *hue hukke hue hukke* call at night.If the call is *bheu bheu,* it is read as an indication of the inauspicious. This time *toyo* is believed to have converted itself into *karaj,* i.e. an inauspicious living being. It is quite alarming. It means that *Jatra bonga* has become dissatisfied and is sending a message to the villagers through a jackal.

When *Raeber Haṛam* (the match-maker) goes to a certain place either in search of a bride or to finalize the negotiations and finds the bird *curhin* coming in his path with its call *urić urić* from the mound of white ants and coming back to the same place, it is considered auspicious as the life of the couple would be prosperous. In case, the bird calling from a dried branch of a tree comes in his path and flies back to the same place, it is considered inauspicious as either the bride or the groom would die soon after marriage.

From these examples, it is observed that some sounds are auspicious or inauspicious in relation to variables like time, space, direction and object. The call of the cock between evening meals and midnight which is inauspicious, is an example of its relationship with time. The call of *curhin cẽṛẽ* from the mound of white ants, which is considered a good omen and the same from the dry branch of the tree which is considered a bad omen, is an example of its relation to places. Further, the call of an oriole which is considered auspicious/inauspicious is an example of its relation to the object (here the bird) and finally the call of a jackal from a particular direction, which is considered inauspicious, is an example of its relation to direction.

Notwithstanding these, the 'auspicious' and the 'inauspicious', as observed by Saraswati (1981), are transcendental categories, each accommodating within itself a great amount of variations and uses. Whatever the variations may be, its central application is unalterable, that is, its transcendental significance remains unchanged. Time, places, objects, directions, events and persons do not inherently possess the quality of the auspicious and the inauspicious. The quality is transferred on each of them in varying contexts. A particular time, a particular event, a particular direction, a particular person or a particular object may be auspicious/ inauspicious in a specific context. The same may, however, not be auspicious/inauspicious in another context. In other words, auspicious/inauspicious has no permanent locus; nothing has a permanent auspicious/inauspicious value (ibid, pp. 23-24). This observation of Saraswati also holds true when the auspicious/ inauspicious sounds of the birds are analyzed by Prasad (1994), after a statistical examination with the help of Chi-Square test having no association with variables like eatable/non-eatable, totemic/non-totemic, sacrificial/non-sacrificial, polluting/non-polluting and intelligent/unintelligent (for details see Tables 1 to 6 in the Appendix.)

In the case of animals it is observed that there is no relation between the variables like eatable-non-eatable, polluting- non-polluting and auspicious-inauspicious sounds. However, the variables like non-totemic, non-sacrificial and intelligent which because of the absence of their contrasting variables like totemic, sacrificial and unintelligent in contingency tables analysed only in terms of percentage values show that in majority of the cases (80 percent) are related to the auspicious and inauspicious sounds (for details see Tables 7 to 12 in the Appendix). This observation, however, does not nullify the above statement that the auspicious and the inauspicious are transcendental categories. If that be so this would have also become valid for the attributes of the birds. This only points to the difference in the perception of the Santhal with regard to birds and animals of the environment which are so due to the closer association and greater utility of the latter. This also holds true in the case of animals where no association is found between variables like eatable-non eatable, polluting-non-polluting and auspicious-inauspicious sounds (see tables 8 and 11 in the appendix). The variables like non-totemic, non-totemic, non-sacrificial and intelligent (as birds having contrasting attributes like totemic, sacrificial and unintelligent are absent) when analyzed are, in 80 per cent of the cases, observed related to the auspicious and inauspicious (see tables 9, 10 and 12 respectively).

What may ultimately be observed from the classification of various sounds under the above categories is that though Santhals apparently make a distinction between *jiweť* (living) and *goć* (dead) elements of nature and other living beings, i.e. animals, birds, and insects, this becomes non-existent in the case of rhythmic sounds, i.e. when an inanimate object is animated or is in use. For example, the term *aṛaṅ* is used to refer to both the sounds produced by man and by musical instruments when played. Again, the distinction between man and other living beings, specially birds, becomes non-existent. The painful cry of human beings and the call of the birds are both referred to as *rak̍*. Thus, it emerges from the discussion that the various categories of sounds among the Santhal are not exclusive but interconnected. This leads to the conclusion that in the Santhal thought, sound inheres the basic principle of differentiation as well as unification of all things of their Universe — spatial and temporal.

## *APPENDIX*

Santhals have three different categories of birds : (a) those whose sound is auspicious (b) those whose sound is inauspicious, and (c) those whose sound is both auspicious and inauspicious. *Potam* (dove) belongs to the first category; *giḍi* (vulture), *kahũ* (crow) and *sim* (fowl) belong to the second category and *pio* (golden oriole), *curhiń* and *laṅtiti* (a large migratory bird) belong to the third category.

The bird *potam* in the first category is eatable, non-totemic, non-sacrificial, non-polluting and unintelligent. Among the birds of the second category, both *giḍi* and *kahũ* are non-eatable, totemic, non-sacrificial, polluting and intelligent. The bird *sim* on the contrary is eatable, non-totemic, sacrificial, non-polluting and unintelligent.

Among the birds of the third category *pio* and *curhiń* are non-eatable and intelligent and *laṅtiti* is eatable and unintelligent. Otherwise, all are non-totemic, non-sacrificial and non-polluting. This information may be summarized in the following tables* :

**Table 1**

| Birds | Sounds | | | |
|---|---|---|---|---|
| | Auspicious | Inauspicious | Both | Total |
| Eatable | 1 | 1 | 1 | 3 |
| Non-eatable | 0 | 2 | 2 | 4 |
| Totemic | 0 | 2 | 0 | 2 |
| Non-totemic | 1 | 1 | 3 | 5 |
| Sacrificial | 0 | 1 | 0 | 1 |
| Non-sacrificial | 1 | 2 | 3 | 6 |
| Polluting | 0 | 2 | 0 | 2 |
| Non-polluting | 1 | 1 | 3 | 5 |
| Intelligent | 0 | 2 | 2 | 4 |
| Unintelligent | 1 | 1 | 1 | 3 |

* If any relation between variables has to be significant, the value of $X^2$ (Chi Square) in these cases, has to be at least 5 at 2 degree of freedom. As this is less than 5 in tables 2-6, 8 and 11 all the variables in tables are independent i.e., they are having no relation to each other.

Now, the information presented in Table 1 may be analysed with the help of a qualitative method to find out whether there exists any relation between the attributes of the birds and the animals and their sounds perceived as auspicious, inauspicious or both by the Santhals. The sample being very small, the Chi-Square test has been applied to find out the association between the attributes. But where the relation between the attributes is obvious it has been discussed in terms of percentage value.

**Table 2**

| Birds | Sounds | | | |
|---|---|---|---|---|
| | Auspicious | Inauspicious | Both | Total |
| Eatable | 1 | 1 | 1 | 3 |
| Non-eatable | 0 | 2 | 2 | 4 |
| Total | 1 | 3 | 3 | 7 |

Result : $X^2 = 1.5$ which is insignificant at 2 degreees of freedom (df). This shows that there is no relation between the attributes.

**Table 3**

| Birds | Sounds | | | |
|---|---|---|---|---|
| | Auspicious | Inauspicious | Both | Total |
| Totemic | 0 | 1 | 0 | 1 |
| Non-eatable | 1 | 2 | 3 | 6 |
| Total | 1 | 3 | 3 | 7 |

Result : $X^2 = 0.7$ which is insignificant at 2 df. Hence there is no relation between the attributes.

**Table 4**

| Birds | Sounds | | | |
|---|---|---|---|---|
| | Auspicious | Inauspicious | Both | Total |
| Sacrificial | 0 | 1 | 0 | 1 |
| Non-sacrificial | 1 | 2 | 3 | 6 |
| Total | 1 | 3 | 3 | 7 |

Result : $X^2 = 1.5$ which is insignificant at 2 df. This shows that there is no relation between the attributes.

**Table 5**

| Birds | Sounds | | | |
|---|---|---|---|---|
| | Auspicious | Inauspicious | Both | Total |
| Polluting | 0 | 2 | 0 | 2 |
| Non-polluting | 1 | 1 | 3 | 5 |
| Total | 1 | 3 | 3 | 7 |

Result : $X^2 = 3.7$ which is insignificant at 2 df; there is no relation between the attributes (table value = 5.99).

**Table 6**

| Birds | Sounds | | | |
|---|---|---|---|---|
| | Auspicious | Inauspicious | Both | Total |
| Intelligent | 0 | 1 | 1 | 2 |
| Unintelligent | 1 | 2 | 2 | 5 |
| Total | 1 | 3 | 3 | 7 |

Result : $X^2 = 0.4$ which is insignificant at 2 df; there is no relation between the attributes.

Further, it is known that the Santhals have two different categories of animals : (a) those whose sound is auspicious, and (b) those whose sound is inauspicious. *Cerceṭeć* (a house-lizard ) belongs to the first category and *khikri* ( a fox), *seta* (a dog), *toyo* (a jackal) and *pusi* (a cat) belong to the second category.

Among these animals, *cerceṭeć, seta, toyo* and *pusi* are non- eatable, non-totemic, non-sacrificial, non-polluting and intelligent. But *khikri* is eatable, non-totemic, non-sacrificial, polluting and intelligent. This information may be summarized in Table 7 :

**Table 7**

| Animals | Sounds | | | |
|---|---|---|---|---|
| | Auspicious | Inauspicious | Both | Total |
| Eatable | 0 | 1 | 0 | 1 |
| Non-eatable | 1 | 3 | 0 | 4 |
| Totemic | 0 | 0 | 0 | 0 |
| Non-totemic | 1 | 4 | 0 | 5 |
| Sacrificial | 0 | 0 | 0 | 0 |
| Non-sacrificial | 1 | 4 | 0 | 5 |
| Polluting | 0 | 1 | 0 | 1 |
| Non-polluting | 1 | 3 | 0 | 4 |
| Intelligent | 1 | 4 | 0 | 5 |
| Unintelligent | 0 | 0 | 0 | 0 |

Now, the information presented in the above tables may be analysed as done before.

**Table 8**

| Animals | Sounds | | | |
|---|---|---|---|---|
| | Auspicious | Inauspicious | Both | Total |
| Eatable | 0 | 1 | 0 | 1 |
| Non-eatable | 1 | 3 | 0 | 4 |
| Total | 1 | 4 | 0 | 5 |

Result : $X^2 = 0.3$ which is insignificant at 2 df. and , therefore, shows no relation between the attributes.

**Table 9**

| Animals | Sounds | | | |
|---|---|---|---|---|
| | Auspicious | Inauspicious | Both | Total |
| Totemic | 0 | 0 | 0 | 0 |
| Non-totemic | 1 (20%) | 4 (80%) | 0 (0%) | 5 (100%) |
| Total | 1 | 4 | 0 | 5 |

From the above table it is observed that there is not a single totemic animal whose sound is either auspicious or inauspicious, i.e. all are non-totemic. Among them 80 percent are having inauspicious sounds. It, therefore, shows that there is a relation between the attributes non-totemic and inauspicious.

**Table 10**

| Animals | Sounds | | | |
|---|---|---|---|---|
| | Auspicious | Inauspicious | Both | Total |
| Sacrificial | 0 | 0 | 0 | 0 |
| Non-sacrificial | 1 (20%) | 4 (80%) | 0 (0%) | 5 (100%) |
| Total | 1 | 4 | 0 | 5 |

From the above table it is observed that all animals having sound either auspicious or inauspicious are non sacrificial, i.e. there is no sacrificial animal. Among them 80 percent have inauspicious sounds. It, therefore, shows that there is a relation between the attributes non-sacrificial and inauspicious.

**Table 11**

| Animals | Sounds | | | |
|---|---|---|---|---|
| | Auspicious | Inauspicious | Both | Total |
| Polluting | 0 | 1 | 0 | 1 |
| Non-polluting | 1 | 3 | 0 | 4 |
| Total | 1 | 4 | 0 | 5 |

Result : $X^2 = 0.3$ which is insignificant and, therefore, shows no relation between the attributes.

**Table 12**

| Animals | Sounds | | | |
|---|---|---|---|---|
| | Auspicious | Inauspicious | Both | Total |
| Intelligent | 1 (20%) | 4 (80%) | 0 (0%) | 5 (100%) |
| Unintelligent | 0 | 0 | 0 | 0 |
| Total | 1 | 4 | 0 | 5 |

From the above table, it is observed that all animals having auspicious and inauspicious sounds are intelligent, but 80 percent of them are inauspicious. This shows that there is a relation between the attributes : intelligent and inauspicious (Source : Prasad, 1994:40-48)

## REFERENCES

Prasad, Onkar, 1994, Santhal Perception of Sound (unpublished). Project report submitted to the Indira Gandhi National Centre for the Arts, New Delhi.

Saraswati, B. N., 1981, Correspondence with Professor T. N. Madan concerning his paper on the categories of Subha and Suddha in Hindu culture : *Newsletter N.K. Bose Memorial Foundation.* 4 (1-2), Jan - Dec. pp. 23-28.

# 8

# BASIC SOUNDS
## A Study in Sound Symbolism of Santhals

*Khageswar Mahapatra*

The Greek 'naturalists', particularly the Stoic philosophers, held the view that the imitative words form the basic set of 'names' from which languages had developed. In view of this theory we may say that onomatopoeic words formed the nucleus of the vocabulary of a language. The concept of 'Basic Language', therefore, is based upon the words which are formed in imitation of the sound associated with the object, actions and feelings. These types of forms have a connotation of somehow illustrating the meaning more immediately than do ordinary speech forms . The fundamental relationship between a word and its meaning is that originally the words were imitative of things they named. This kind of relationship between the constituent sounds of words and their meaning is 'Sound Symbolism'

All languages are systems of symbols. The symbolism involved in linguistic communication is of two types : (i) iconic/ expressive and (ii) arbitrary/referential. The forms of the first category are onomatopoeic or echoic , whereas those of the second category are arbitrarily construed with no direct or indirect connection with the phonetic structure of the forms. In the English language the word "cuckoo", for example, illustrates the Ono words and "dog" an arbitary verbal symbol. Despite direct phonetic imitation, however, Ono words always fit into the phonetic system of a particular language. The barking sound of a dog is described in speech communities differently such as, *bho, bheu, bhyau, bhu,* etc., and this action is named *bhuk* (to bark ). This aspect reflects the phonoaesthetic sense of the linguistic groups. Thus, sound symbolism and phonoaestheme of a speech community seem to be interrelated.

The formation of Ono and Echo words is regulated by certain rules and devices. One of these principles is reduplication. One type of reduplication is total repetition of the base morpheme (e.g. *khoṭ khoṭ*) and the other type is partial duplication (e.g. *kha ṭar khaṭ*). But the type of reduplication with a change in the base morpheme at the repetitive slot is called echo formation (*khaṭ-khāṭ*). The derivation of all these three types of forms are phonologically conditioned to a large extent.

## II

The Santhals, like all other tribal communities, have their distinct ethnic identity which is clearly marked in their language. The ethnography of a tribe is never complete without reference to the ethno-linguistic aspects of their culture.The basic features of human verbal behaviour are preserved in the tribal languages and come out distinctly in the vocabulary, sound symbolism , grammatical structures and derivations.

Santhali, the ancestral speech of the Santhal tribe, is remarkably rich in sound symbolism . It has a large corpus of words which have been formed or generated in imitation of the natural sounds produced by the referent objects or actions. The goat, for example, is called/*merom*/, the owl/*kokor*/, the heron/*ko*/, the stream flows/*saḍ-saḍ*/, the wind blows/ *sayaṇ-sayaṇ*/, the door closes/ *sarphaḍ-sarphaḍ*/, to kiss is /coˀ/.

There are five categories of words which have phonoaesthetic functions :

1. Onomatopoeic - / *roṭ-roṭ*/ sound of grinding
2. Echo - / *cabar-cubur*/ sound of wading through water
3. Repetitive - / *mẽ - mẽ* / sound of the goat's call

4. Reduplicative - / *hehe ko. e-ko.*ə crackle of the hen
5. Tag - / *Saḍguru-baḍguru*/ sound of sipping liquid food

The process of derivation of the above categories of words is more or less systematic and the formations are governed by a set of phonological rules, such as,

əC > əCa ən - əna
aCaC > aCiC apan-apin
CəC > əCəC kos-kəs.
Cica > CaCe jiha-jahe
CeC > CeCe ret-rete
eCa uCu era+uru (C=consonant)

The Santhali words of sound symbolism broadly designate things, manners, quality or actions. From the semantic point of view, such words entail different shades of meaning, however vague or marginal they may be. Many nouns, verbs, adjectives and adverbs, are basically derived forms, the bases being the sounds associated with them . The natural sounds signal meanings which form the base of a language, the speech of a community of autochthonous people.

Pandit Raghunath Murmu, the famous inventor of Ol Chiki, a script for Santhali, while shaping the alphabets for the Santhali sounds, worked with the conviction that when there was a name, there must be a form. He designed the letters of his script in imitation of the objects, actions and feelings. The sound symbolism of the Santhals is represented in the Ol Chiki graphemes (see Appendix).

**OL CHIKI**

## OL CHIKI

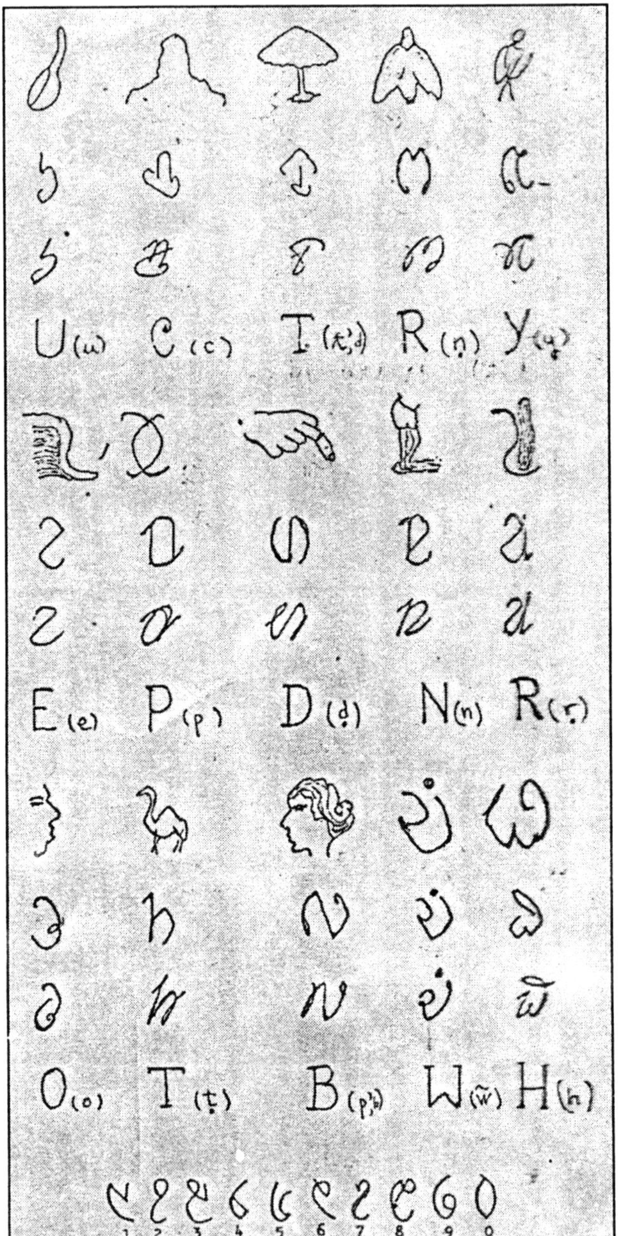

APPENDIX

## SELECT LIST OF THE FORMS OF SOUND SYMBOLISM OF THE SANTHALS

1. Names based on sounds* :

| *sound* | - | *name* | - | *meaning* |
|---|---|---|---|---|
| huhu | - | hʌy | - | wind |
| cẽ cẽ | - | cen̥e | - | bird |
| rẽ rẽ | - | rerenj | - | cricket |
| kAˀ kAˀ | - | kAˀ | - | heron |
| mẽ mẽ | - | merAm | - | goat |
| cAˀ cAˀ | - | cAˀ | - | kiss |
| tud tud | - | tud | - | woodpecker |
| Bhu Bhu | - | Bhuḷ | - | dog (male) |
| Pa ṭ Pa ṭ | - | Piṭna | - | mallet |
| ta : ta : | - | haṭa : | - | winnowing fan |

2. *Onomatopoeic forms :*

| | |
|---|---|
| gisir gisir – adv | The sound produced when scratching the body continuously at the time of itching sensation |
| gubuṛ gubuṛ – | Sound of a musical instrument known as *dhAmsa* |
| guhuṛ guhuṛ – adv. | The sound of a musical instrument known as *nagra* |
| Ciyap Ciyap. – adv | The noise made by the chicken |

* Explanatory note on sings / symbols :
/ ? / Glottal stop
/ + / Tag words
/ — / Syllable boundary, pause
/ . / Grave
/ : / Length
/ ~ / Nasalisation
/ A̠, ṭ, ḍ, ṛ, ṇ, ḷ / Cerebral stops

| | |
|---|---|
| JhawA JhawA – adv. | The barking sound of many dogs at the same time |
| ṭhaḷA : ṭhaḷA: / ṭhaḷa : ṭhaḷa | The sound of the pestle while pounding |
| ḍabu ḍabu – adv. | The sound of the *dhamsa* drum |
| da da - adv. | The sound of tambour |
| parat parat - adv. | The sound produced when someone is beaten with a cane |
| phASA phAS A-adv. | The sound of indistinct words coming out of the mouth |

3. *Echoic forms :*

| | |
|---|---|
| ḍaraj ḍuruj - adj. | The sound made by the pigs while searching for their food |
| ḍahab ḍuhub - adv. | A type of sound produced while walking |
| tuḍhi ruḍhi - adv. | (1) The disorderly sound or tune<br>(2) To play a flute in a disorderly manner |
| raṭa paṭa - adv. | Rattling or clattering sound produced at the time of pulling wattle |
| raga baga/vaga - adv. | The rattling or clattering sound produced when birds, reptiles (snakes, etc.) move on the dry leaves fallen on the ground |
| rigAyA rAgAyA -adv. | The sound produced when frying parched paddy |
| ruḷa; ruḷi - adv. | Hard/rough sound |
| regha reghi - adv. | To sing a song in a loud voice |

| | |
|---|---|
| sa su - adv. | Gasping with hissing sound, hissing noise produced at the time of gasping |
| hak-A pak-A - adv. | The repeated crying sound of a bird |
| hanar jhanar - adv. | Used to express the tinkling/tringling/ jingling sound (as of ornaments, anklets or a similar object) |

4. *Reduplicative forms :*

| | |
|---|---|
| uc ucu - adv. - | Rising higher and higher (such as mountain), the act of elevating |
| unj unj - v. | To insist (on), the act of obstinacy |
| ehel ehel - adj. | Stout (man ) strong and stout, fatty |
| KAṭap Kaṭap - v. | To knock down (with a stick), strike with the knuckle, warn |
| Ka. ṭij Ka. ṭij - adj. | Little (pieces), very small pieces. To cut into pieces, to make into small pieces (by hand) |
| KuḍA KuḍA - adv. | Bending down the head and back |
| gAi gAi - adv. | To itch |
| gayur gayur - adv. | Hanging, swinging, danglingly |
| gir gir - adv. | Angrily, being enraged, to fret and fume |
| Cuk Cuk - v. | To love, show tenderness, affection or love (uttering the word Cu Cu) |
| Cukuc Cukuc - adv. | (To) come or go limpingly and slowly |

# 9

# FORMATION OF OL CHIKI SCRIPT AND PROCESS OF ITS TRANSMISSION

*Shyam Sundar Mohapatra*

---

The Ol Chiki script invented by Pandit Raghunath Murmu, was an epoch-making invention, which provided appropriate writing symbols to the Santhals. The scripts of most other major Indian languages originated in the hoary past and the story of their origin has been a matter of historical research. But the Ol Chiki has been invented only 70 years back. Pandit Raghunath Murmu first conceptualized the script in the 1920s and gave it the final shape in the 1940s. Though a recent phenomenon, the creation of the script has been associated with some myths and play of supernatural powers. Moreover, the characters of the script are not merely an imitation of those current in other languages around. Most of them are inventions of Pandit Raghunath Murmu. The alphabet is also quite limited in size consisting of only 30 characters and is convenient both for printing and writing (Appendix-1). The script, therefore, provides sufficient scope for study from the following points: 1. (a) Origin of Ol Chiki script : myths and beliefs; (b) Depiction of natural, physical environment in the characters of Ol Chiki and their relationship with everyday life of the Santhal; symbolism in shape of the alphabet and the pronounced sound; 2. Association of script with ritual drawing; 3. Methods of transmitting Ol Chiki script.

**Myths and Beliefs**

Myths occur in a society where beliefs, rather than reasoning, reign supreme. The Santhal society, in the 1920s, (when Western education had not spread so much among its members) was prone to superstitions and myths. When something uncommon was achieved by a member of such a society, it was attributed to some supernatural power, and many myths cropped up. Even the performers of such deeds believed in supernatural blessings. So when Pandit Raghunath Murmu invented the script, the folk around him believed it to be something supernatural and myths were woven to explain the phenomenon.

Rameswar Murmu presents two myths regarding the origin of the Ol Chiki script (Murmu, 1988). According to one, the script originated with the creation of the earth. Before this , lightning created fire in the sky from which the first letter "A" originated. With the formation of earth, "at" appeared. The first five characters, in this way, appeared from the first basic elements, namely, earth, water, fire, air and sky. This conception is similar to a Hindu myth in which *Om* is held as the Supreme Being (*Akshar Brahma*).

Murmu further informs that when Pandit Raghunath was studying in the third standard, the Santhal gods, *Bidu* and *Chandan*, came to him in a dream and told him that if he worshipped them, he would find the script. From then onwards he started worshipping these gods.When he grew to be young, he went to the mountain *Kaphiburu* alone and worshipped *Bidu* and *Chandan* there. The gods showed him the script in a dream. The purpose of the first myth is clear. It presents the script as primordial and sacred. Emergence of this myth may be due to a feeling of reverence for the script on account of its magical power.

The second myth presents the script as divine. It resolves a binary opposition between two beliefs : (1) The Ol Chiki script was invented by some human being, and (2) The script was of divine origin. The myth suggests that the script was a divine gift to a blessed man. Common man considers anything extraordinary to be the doings of gods. Even great authors and inventors believe that their deeds were the result of God's blessings. Such faith among the Santhals has given rise to myths regarding Ol Chiki too.

### Nature characters of Ol Chiki

A Santhal scholar, Rameswar Murmu (1988), who discusses the making of Ol Chiki script, shows how Pandit Raghunath Murmu might have derived all the characters from familiar sources. Sitakant Mahapatra (1986) has enlisted the sources of the characters as collected from an interview with Pandit Raghunath and his son. There are some minor differences in the two versions. The following are some of the main sources of the script, according to the two versions :

(a) Natural :

According to Rameswar Murmu the first five characters of Ol Chiki came from the five basic elements as indicated below :

Ạ from *Sengel* (Fire) ᱚ<br>
Ạt from *Hasa* (soil) ᱛ<br>
Ạk' from *Dak* (water) ᱜ<br>
Ạn from *Hoi* (air) ᱝ<br>
Ạl from *Soon* (sky) ᱞ

Some connections between the five characters and the five basic elements can , of course, be traced either in the shape of the characters or the sound they represent. The character Ạ is in the shape of burning fire, the character Ạt is round representing the earth surrounded by the horizon, the character Ạk' echoes the sound *daḱ* meaning water, though Rameswar Murmu states that the shape of the character represents an open mouth vomiting and Pandit Raghunath explains it as a sketch of a bird bearing the same name.

The character Ạn represents upper and lower lips with air coming out and the character Ạl, which means writing, is associated with the sky or heaven certainly as something divine.

Some more characters derived from Nature

| | | | |
|---|---|---|---|
| ᱪ | uch | - | Peak of hill |
| ᱮ | e | - | Over flowing river changing course |
| ᱤ | i | - | Bending tree |
| ᱫ | ud | - | Mushroom; ᱫ (the same letter in primers) |
| ᱴ | ot | - | Hump of a camel; ᱴ (the same letter in primers) |
| ᱠ | Ạk | - | A bird |
| ᱬ | Un | - | Picture of a flying bee |

(b) Physical Environment :

| | | | |
|---|---|---|---|
| ᱥ | (ish) | - | Shape of a plough |
| ᱨ | (ir) | - | Figure of a sickle |
| ᱩ | (u) | - | Shape of a vessel for preparing food |
| ᱟ | (A) | - | Shape of a man using a spade in the field |
| ᱷ | (oh) | - | Figure of a person throwing something with one hand |

(c) Common Postures of everyday life :

| | | | |
|---|---|---|---|
| ᱡ | (Aj) | - | Shape of spreading hands |
| ᱢ | (Am) | - | Indicating 'you' |
| ᱣ | (Au) | - | Opening of lips |
| ᱦ | (ih) | - | Hands up |
| ᱧ | (inj) | - | Pointing to oneself |
| ᱭ | (Ui) | - | A man bending towards the ground |

| | | | |
|---|---|---|---|
| ᱯ | (ep) | - | A person receiving something with both hands from another |
| ᱰ | (ed) | - | Shape of a man with two legs stretching towards his chest and mouth |
| ᱱ | (en) | - | One working in bending position |
| ᱲ | (er) | - | One avoiding an arrow with one hand |
| ᱳ | (o) | - | Shape of opened lips |
| ᱵ | (oub) | - | Shape of curly hair |
| ᱶ | (oun) | - | Nasalized |

It is obvious that the characters are derived from nature including the five basic elements, physical environment and a number of them from common postures of everyday life. However, it can be noticed that some of the favourite objects and animals have not been accommodated in the alphabet. For example, the animals dog, pig, buffalo are absent though the camel had to be brought in for the sound "ṭ". Similarly, though the domestic bird swan has been entertained for its sound (Ak), the cock has been left out. Thus the sources of characters have been very selective in consideration of the sounds to be represented. The difficulty in bringing favourite objects can be realized when we consider the process of formation of the Ol Chiki script.

## Symbolism in the Shape of Characters and the Pronounced Sound

Scholars point out a close relationship in the symbolized, pronounced sounds and their meaning in each case. The interview conducted by Sitakant Mahapatra with Pandit Raghunath Murmu confirms the fact. In some cases, of course, the relation is very clear as in the following examples :

| Symbol | Pronounced Sound | Meaning of the pronounced sound | Significance of the shape of the symbol |
|---|---|---|---|
| ᱚ | At | Earth | Round as earth |
| ᱤ | Ir | To reap | Sickle with an object within its compass |
| ᱩ | Ut' | Mushroom | Picture of mushroom |
| ᱥ | Is | Plough | Picture of a plough |
| ᱪ | Uc | Something raised up | Peak of a hill |
| ᱴ | Oṭ | Camel | Resembles the hump of camel |
| ᱳ | On | To blow air | Figure of passing wind between two lips |

Though it is claimed that the shape of all the symbols in each case have an affinity with the meaning of the pronounced sound, at least in some cases it is not convincing. Here are some examples :

| Symbol | Sound | Meaning of the sound | Shape |
|---|---|---|---|
| ᱦ | (Ih) | A word expressing terror | Action of a man in terror |
| ᱭ | (Uy) | Response to a call from a distance | Action of hands in answering such a call |
| ᱰ | (Ed) | To point out a place | Fist with a finger pointing to a particular place |

It is noteworthy that there are some differences in the meaning of pronounced sounds suggested by two scholars, Pandit Raghunath himself and Rameswar Murmu as shown below :

| Symbol | Pronounced Sound | Meaning given by Pundit Raghunath | Meaning given by Rameswar Murmu |
|---|---|---|---|
| ᱜ | (Ạk') | Sound of opened mouth as if to vomit | Shape of a bowl containing water |
| ᱠ | (Ak) | Rough sketch of a bird bearing the name 'Ak' | Sound of swan |
| ᱣ | (Aw) | A word expressing curiosity and amazement. Modified from a position of hands expressing the feelings | Opening of lips |
| ᱭ | (Uy) | Response to a call from distance modified from actions of hands in answering such a call | A man bending towards the ground |
| ᱰ | (Ed) | To point out a place | Shape of a man with two legs stretching towards his chest and mouth |

In spite of a difference of opinion with regard to the pronounced sound of the symbols, it is to be admitted that most of the symbols have meaning corresponding to their shapes and pronounced sounds . Again whatever be the sources of symbols, according to Santhal scholars, some resemblance of the symbols with those of English and neighbouring Oriya, Bengali and Devanagri characters also can be noticed as indicated below.

| Santhali | English | Bengali | Devanagri | Oriya | Remarks |
|---|---|---|---|---|---|
| ᱛ (Ạt) | 0(0) | | | 0(t) | |
| ᱜ (ẠK) | | Figure five (৫) | | | |
| ᱝ (Ạm) | | | अ (A) | | |
| ᱞ (Ạl) | p(p) | | | | |
| ᱠ (Ak) | b(b) | | | | |
| ᱢ (Am) | U | | | |  (Am in Santhal primer) |
| ᱣ (Au) | (ih) | (Li) ঌ | | | |
| ᱦ (ih) | W | | | | |
| ᱧ (inj) | q | | | | |
| ᱩ (u) | | | | ଉ (ଉ) also the figure six (୬) | |
| ᱬ (un) | M | | | | |
| ᱮ (e) | | Z (e) | | | |
| ᱰ (ed) | S (Placed horizontally) | | | | |
| ᱳ (O) | | | | ଓ (o) | |
| ᱷ (oh) | w | | | | |

Inspite of a resemblance of the symbols to those of English and some Indian scripts, the originality of Pandit Raghunath in conceiving of Ol Chiki must be admitted.

## Principles of Formation of the Santhal Script and Method of its Transmission

Pandit Raghunath Murmu, an educated man, conceived of the Santhal script systematically. Clearly he has followed some principles in the process which appear to be as follows :

1. First he sorted out the vowel sounds which came to be 6 in number.
2. Then he sorted out the consonants which came to be 24 in number.
3. As consonants cannot be pronounced separately, he combined each vowel with four consonants in such a way that each combination gave some meaning.
4. He shaped the symbols according to the meaning of the pronounced sound of each consonant as well as vowels.

## Association of Ol Chiki with Ritual Drawings

On the basis of information obtained from Pandit Raghunath and the opinion of Rameswar Murmu, we have shown earlier that the symbols are mainly derived from nature, physical environment and every day life of Santhals. Their relation with ritual drawings is also worth noting. But a comparison of such drawings (Appendix-2 (a) (b) ) with the script does not show any striking resemblance. Only the round figures drawn as home of gods are similar to a character "Ot" which is also round. But a round figure in an alphabet or numericals is a universal phenomenon. Hence with regard to the sources of the symbols, the information given by Pandit Raghunath may be accepted (Appendix-3).

## Transmission of the Script

Though there are 30 characters in the Ol Chiki alphabet, six of them are designed in such a way that each of them represents two sounds if used reversely. Therefore, practically 24 letters are to be learnt. As discussed above, each symbol has a meaning and the symbols correspond to the pronounced sounds of them. Moreover, the symbols have some pictorial quality derived from natural as well as physical environment. In this way, the alphabet has been helpful for easy transmission. Since the process of writing is also simple (Appendix-4) it needs no special way of transmission even to children.

## Conclusion

In conclusion it may be enough to say that some myths have cropped up around the Ol Chiki script which is an ingenious invention of Pandit Raghunath. Very carefully he has derived the characters from nature, physical environment and everyday life of the Santhal. He has been able to maintain affinity between sound and symbol. The very ingenuity in shaping the symbols and arrangement of the script has been greatly helpful in transmission of the script.

# APPENDIX-1

## The Ol Chiki

Characters For Printing — Characters For Writing

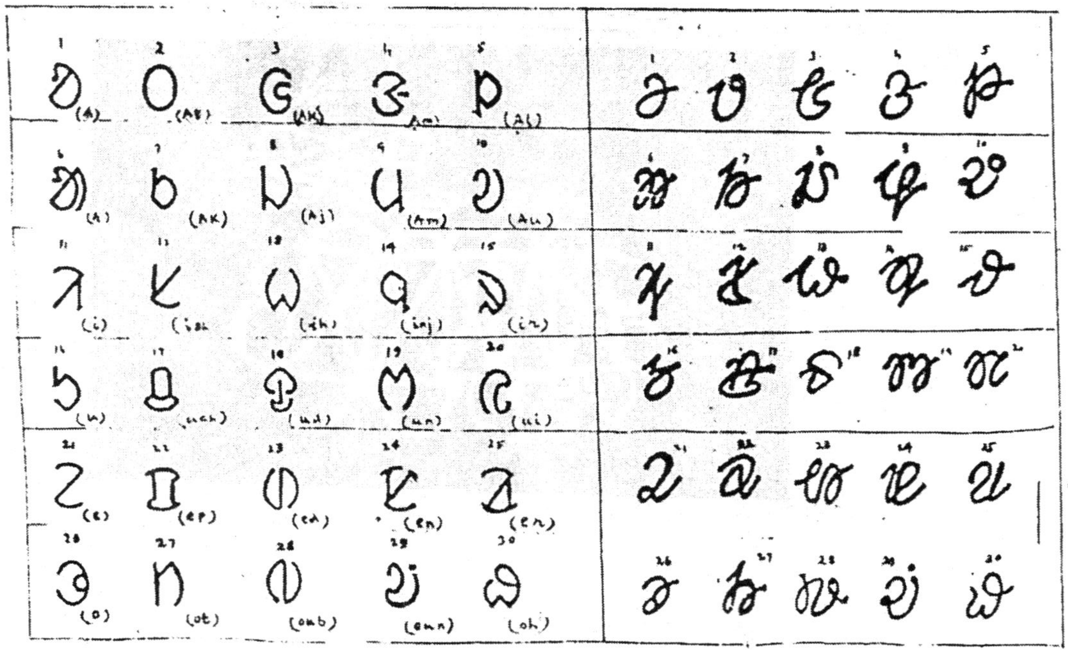

*APPENDIX-2 (a)*

**Santhal ritual drawing from a collection of Onkar Prasad for IGNCA**

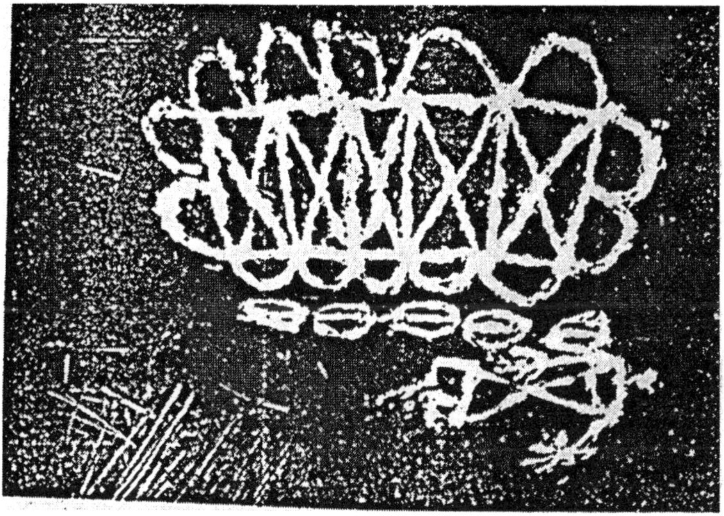

*APPENDIX-2 (b)*

**Santhal ritual drawing from a collection of Onkar Prasad for IGNCA**

*APPENDIX-3*

**Sources of the Ol Chiki Script**

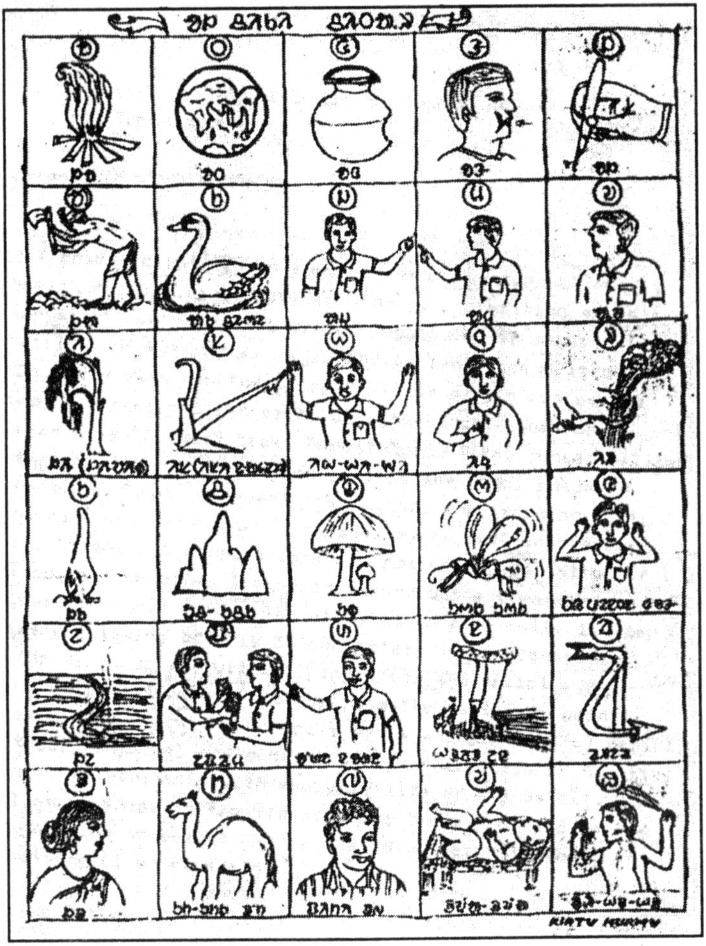

*APPENDIX-4*

**The Process of Writing Ol Chiki**

Characters For Printing | Characters For Writing

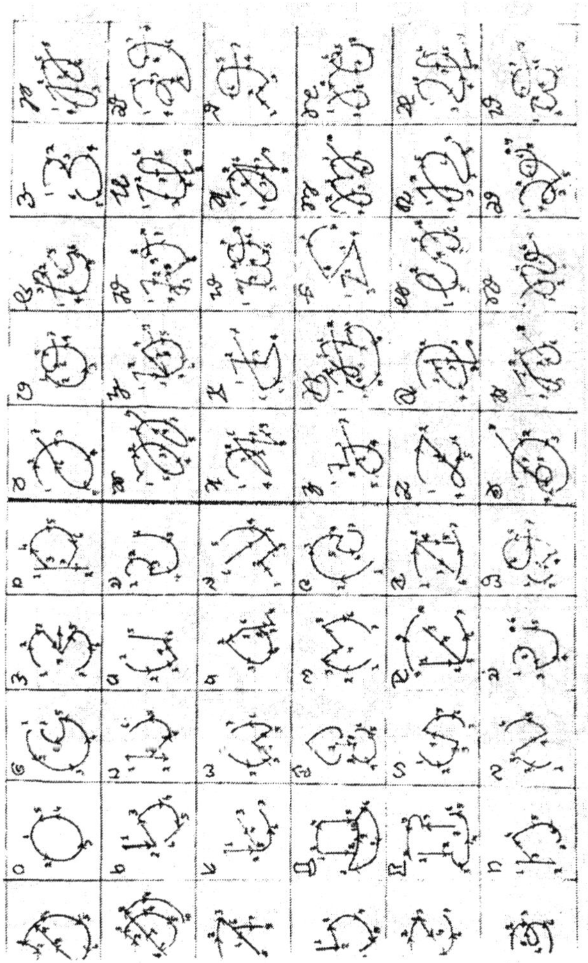

## REFERENCES

Mahapatra, Sitakant, 1986, *Modernization and Ritual Identity and Change in Santal Society,* Oxford University Press.

Murmu, Raghunath, *Ol Chemet* (A Santali Primer, 12th edition), Orissa Adivasi Socio-Educational & Cultural Association.

Murmu, Rameswar, 1988, *Ol Chikireyah Galhan.*

# 10

# SANTHAL LANGUAGE AND CULTURE

*Chaitanya Prasad Majhi*

---

Language and culture are the main constituents of the identity of a people. Language develops with the educational progress of a people and cultural boundary expands with the changing taste of the people. It is necessary to evolve a standard measure in order to make a proper appreciation of the subject in question. The language and culture are two ingredients of any society, be it 'modern' or 'primitive' which could be used as yardsticks to determine the 'level' of civilization of that community.

While language, which is the vehicle of thought, expression and means of communication among the members of that particular social group, has its own domain or boundary to hold the people together making for their identity, the culture has a tendency to scale the language barrier and expand its frontiers slowly by accepting foreign or alien ones which appeal to its people. Some conservative families of our country who were against Western culture, for example, slowly accepted the Western ways of life. Initially there was an attitude of abhorrence to the Western ways of life among the orthodox Hindus. They did not like their young daughters to wear jeans and garments used by the boys. Some were very averse to taking food or tea in restaurants. In course of time, however, the walls of protest got demolished. Now, the entire cultural life of our country has undergone a sea change.

Culture is inherited from the past. It includes the entire lifestyle of a people, their dress, ornaments, food habits, customs and traditions, religious beliefs and rites, social customs, marriage traditions, music and dance. These constituents of culture are true for the modern societies as also for the tribal societies.

The language of a nation or of a community binds it together making it distinct from others. The more the cultural life of the people expands its frontiers, the more they rise towards higher realms of civilization, towards perfection. The language, on the other hand, is a mirror which reflects the total cultural world of a community. Its literature, which is enriched by education and learning of the community, imagination of the poets, writers and artists holds together the entire expanse of the cultural canvas from the past to the present and gives a new twist to the cultural life of the community.

The Santhals belong to the tribal stock of people spread over Bihar, West Bengal, Orissa and Assam. Although they are a much written about people, there is a scope to study them from closer quarters. The missionaries have studied them and their dialect from the standpoint of spreading Christianity among them. Many aspects of Santhal heritage and culture, therefore, remain unexplored till date.

The origin of the Santhals is shrouded in mystery. They were called 'aborigines' for a long time in the past. Some anthropologists classify them as Australoids. Rev. P. O. Bodding, who tried to delve deep into their language and culture says that the ancestors of these people came as imigrants to Champa, possibly a country to the north-east of the present Chota Nagpur plateau; prior to which the Santhals, Mundas, Birhors and Kurmis were called by the name of Kherwar.

It might be mentioned that *sat* has been explained as derived from Sanskrit *smant* (bordering) so that the term Santhal might really mean, 'a man of the border', 'a borderer'. The epic of *Ramayana* tells us how Lord Rama was assisted by Hanuman, the monkey king. It is of interest in this connection to remember that the Hindus, even to this day, occasionally call the Santhals, monkeys. Further the Santhal tradition states that their ancestors assisted King Rama in his war with Ravana. Although the conjecture made by Rev. Bodding is not based on a conclusive proof, it has an element of truth in it. Some further evidence would go in support of Rev. Bodding's point. Among the Santhals the names of Rama, Lakshmana, Sita, Bharata, Chatura (Shatrughna), Dasaratha, etc., are preponderant. The Santhals invariably inherit the names of their ancestors. Hence, it can be inferred that they lived in the days of the *Ramayana*. Of course, few traces of names here and there cannot lead us to a conclusive proof to trace the origin of the Santhals. Further research in this regard is necessary.

Pandit Raghunath Murmu, a distinguished writer of Santhal language, who founded the Ol Chiki script has a different story to tell regarding the origin of the Santhals. He cites a legend prevalent among the community which is often recited on the occasion of marriage ceremonies of the Santhals in the form of a *binti* song. It is based on age-old traditions and it needs to be examined by experts for allegorical meanings. Pandit Murmu has described the story in his epic poem *Hital*. It is a long story. But I give only the gist of it here. According to the legend *Dharma*, the first Lord of creation of the Universe, created *Maran Buru* and *Jahi Rangi* — *Adi Purusha* and *Shakti* (first man and female energy) in the forms of winds with infinite velocities. The forces of winds created a whirlwind of a tremendous magnitude which produced fire, lightning and explosions. From these explosions, the Universal celestial heavenly bodies like sun, stars, planets, earth and moon were born. They were hurled into their respective orbits on the wishes of the Almighty. A cyclonic storm with rain and thunder submerged the earth under the waters of the sea. *Maran Buru* then created two heavenly swans, one male and the other female. These birds first created the beings that would live in the sea. Then, slowly the surface of the Earth appeared. *Hihiri*, a very high precipice came out first and later *Pipiri*, a plain landmass beneath the *Hihiri* appeared. The heavenly birds created the plants, trees, land animals, birds and all other creatures of the land. They also created all the living beings on the wishes of *Maran Buru*. But his desire to create was not satisfied. He, therefore, ordered the birds to create human beings —the highest creatures. The birds built a nest in a *Karam* tree near the seashore. The female bird laid two eggs in a nest. From the eggs, two human babies were born : one boy and the other a girl. The babies were named *Pilcus* by *Maran Buru*. The parent birds brought up the babies on milk produced from their beaks. This became possible as *Maran Buru* desired it. The children got down from the nest when they were able to crawl through a ladder of soft *sirm* grass. The other birds, who used to come to the *Karam* tree, became friendly with the *Pilcus* and brought ripe soft fruits for them. When the babies learnt to eat fruits by themselves the heavenly swans returned to their abode. *Maran Buru* remained on the Earth to preserve his creation. He loved *Pilcus* the most. He constantly watched and guarded them against dangers. He taught them to talk, of course, in Santhali. They called him *abba* (father). They became adults. *Maran Buru* realized that they did not have sex. One day he expressed the desire to drink *rasi* (alcoholic drink) from their hands. He taught them the process of making the *rasi*. When the *rasi* was ready *Maran Buru* appeared. He asked them to offer him one cup (made from Sal leaf) full of *rasi* ritually. They followed his directions. *Maran Buru* took his share and disappeared. The *Pilcus* drank the remaining *rasi*, which overpowered them completely. They lost control under the influence of liquor and made love at night. Next morning *Maran Buru* came to see them. The *Pilcus* had not come out till then. They were afraid of showing their faces because they thought that they had committed a wrong. They were also ashamed of being naked. *Maran Buru* asked them to come out. From inside the hut, they apologized for having done some wrong. He consoled them that they had not committed any wrong. Then they came out covering their loins with Sal leaves tied together with strings. But *Maran Buru* had vanished from the scene. He was not to be found. Only his voice came, that he would come to their help whenever they called him. Lady *Pilcu* conceived for the first time and delivered a male child in due course. The *Pilcus* were puzzled when it was born as they had not known how babies were born. They prayed to *Maran Buru* for help. *Maran Buru* responded and told them the way they should observe post-natal rituals. The Santhals follow the practice of post-natal rituals in the manner told by their Supreme Lord even till today.

The *Pilcus'* first child grew into a boy. They wanted a child again. They followed the same process. In course of time, *Pilcus* had seven sons and seven daughters who married each other when they grew up. They founded the seven clans of Santhal tribes, which are : *Hansdak, Murmu, Soren, Kisku, Hembram, Marndi* and *Tudu*. This was the last marriage among the agnates. *Maran Buru* imposed prohibition on marriage among the agnates from then onwards.

According to Pandit Murmu, *Hihiri* is the other name of the Himalaya mountains and *Pipiri* is the land between the Himalayas and the Sea which otherwise means India. The Santhals are, therefore, the original inhabitants of India which is known as *singh ot* by the Santhals.

## Santhal Lifestyle

I have tried to trace the origin of the Santhals for a purpose. Santhals, are orthodox people with a tendency to cling to the past. Their religion *Sarna* is based on Nature's worship. *Maran Buru*, their Creator has said, "I am everywhere, in every form". Therefore, they worship the trees in the *jaher* by installing *Jaher era*, *Maneka* and *Lita Thakur* under the trees. The Santhals believe that the mountains and the hills are the home of gods and goddesses *(bongas)*. The *bongas* live everywhere. The *Sima sala bongas* are worshipped either at the starting of the cultivation of a plot of land or at the time of harvest. Event of *Sima sala bonga* starts when a ploughman is bitten by a poisonous snake while ploughing a particular plot for a number of times or falls sick during ploughing of that plot. The owner is led to believe that the *Sima sala bonga* is aggrieved and the propitiating of the *bonga* starts by sacrificing a poultry bird. The Santhals are extremely superstitious people.

They believe that the world is full of spirits — good as well as evil. The good spirits are known as *bongas*. They are said to respond to the call of mankind when worshipped by any individual or the village community and bring prosperity and well-being to the caller. The evil spirits, the *Bhoot-bongas*, on the other hand, cause harm to men. They have a belief that very often illness and disease are caused by their influence. Hence *Ojha* (witch-doctor) is required to drive away the evil sirit.

They observe various religious festivals throughout the year starting from the festival of *Baha* which coincides with the spring in (month of March or April), *Erok bonga* seed sowing festival is in the month of May or June, *Ashadiya bonga* rain invoking festival in the month of July; *Gomha* festival in the month of August or September as per the *tithi*; *Dasain* festival concides with *Durga puja; Sohrae* festival sometime coincides with Deepavali; *makar* festival in the month of January and *magha bonga* falls in the month of March. Some festivals are of course coterminus with Hindu festivals while others are not observed at the same time in all the villages of a locality.

Besides the traditional festivals, there are other social functions on the occasion of birth, marriage and death which are attended by the villagers as a matter of practice and social custom. No invitation is necessary; merely informing the village *Manjhi* or "godet" is enough.

The Santhals, therefore, live as well-knit communiy. A village of Santhals is easily identified from the style of the houses and the wall decorations which are simple but often resembling with each other. The village invariably has a sacred grove or *jaher* on its outskirts which is a place of worship of the *bongas*, the village deities and a *gosan* in the village street for the worship of ancient *Manjhi Hadam*.

Every religious or social function is celebrated by the community with drinks, dance and music. Each function has a particular type of song, music and dance forms although the sound and musical instruments remain the same. The songs are generally inherited from the past and carry little or no message for the community. They are short couplets. During the marriage functions love songs are sometimes composed by the youth on the spot. On the religious occasions, the dance and music starts from the place of worship — *jaher* and are concluded at the village wrestling ground or *akhada* which is situated in front of the village headman's house. The sound instruments like *tumdak* (slightly different from mridangama), *tamak, chadchadi* (drums) and the musical instrument *banam*, an indigenous violin and *triyau* the flute are played. Any departure from the old practice is objected to and at times considered an offence by the elders of the village. Of course, the penalty for an infringement may be merely a pot of ricebeer for the villagers. The system has to work according to the prescribed manner unalloyed by the march of time.

The Santhali language has a striking resemblance with the Sanskrit language. There are three grammatical numbers as in Sanskrit, i.e. singular, dual and plural. As a matter of illustration, forms of the pronouns are given below :

| | | *Singular* | *Dual* | *Plural* |
|---|---|---|---|---|
| Sanskrit first person | : | aham | abam | bayam |
| Santhali first person | : | ingz (alang) | alingz | abo |
| Sanskrit second person | : | twom | yubam | yuyam |
| Santhali second person | : | am | abimn | ape |
| Sanskrit third person | : | saw | tau | te |
| Santhali third person | : | ac' | akin | ako |
| (Other than human beings) | : | uni | unkin | unku |

Some Sanskrit words are found in the Santhali language which establishes the fact that the Santhals had contact with Sanskrit speaking people in the ancient times. But it is a paradox that the language has remained largely unchanged though it is very old. It is probably because the Santhals preferred to remain within their own world for fear of being exploited by the more clever communities.

**The Village**

The entire social system of the Santhals is controlled by the village council (*Manjhi-Manchor*). Santhal village nominates its headman (*Manjhi*), his deputy (*Jog Manjhi*) and his secretary

(*Godet*). All the villagers become the members of the Village Council. There of course, is a village priest (*Naeke*) for worshipping of the village deities. The village council acts as an institution to settle all commual disputes of the village. The rigidity with which the customary law of the community is enforced by the village council apparent from the observations made by W.G.Archer in his monumental treatise, *Tribal Law and Justice.* Santhal law, as now exists, is not an arbitrary creation of an individual. In giving it a logic and a pattern, each grade of tribal council plays a part. Santhal law is actually a synthesis of tribal attitudes expressed through a hierarchy of tribal courts. The first of these assemblies is the village community. This body is the original court of tribal justice and in all disputes it is the first to intervene. Its duty is to see that the rites of birth, initiation and death, the conduct of the year's festivals, the laws of exogamy and cohabitation are duly observed. It ensures that the principles of the laws are followed, it maintains civil rights and in many cases it acts as a court of registration. It revolves around seven village officials and while in point of law these are only its servants, the administration of the village, maintenance and making of its law depend on their integrity and influence. The Santhals have prescribed certain customary rules which are to be followed for marriage, divorce and inheritance by the members of the community. Marriage among the agnates or outside the Santhal community considered as an offence calls for penalty of ex-communication. There are many laws which impose restrictive practices in the customs of the community. The members of the community follow these laws rigidly for fear of punishment. The boundary walls of the community are inviolable and even the 'enlightened' among the Santhals fear to tread on them. This is the sole reason why the community still retains its culture without any desire to accept acculturation and wind of change in their day-to-day lifestyle.

A turning point in the cultural life of Santhals seems to have come after the Independence. Pandit Raghunath Murmu took the community by a storm when he invented Ol Chiki — the Santhali script for its language. He pleaded strongly that since the community was spread over Bihar, West Bengal, Orissa and Assam the regional scripts were not suitable for the language and they cannot overcome the communication barrier. Ol Chiki script is the only medium to establish links between the people of the community. His arguments were very convincing to the Santhal people. He published his books in the Santhali script. A printing press was established to publish a fortnightly Santhali magazine, *Sagen Sakam*. An unprecedented enthusiasm overtook the Santhals. The educated Santhal people learnt the script by themselves to spread the message. Since the people knew the language, it became easier for them to learn the script through the key book *Tribhasi* and could read other books written in Santhali scripts without much difficulty. Pandit Murmu had earlier published his famous drama "Bidu Chandan" in Oriya and Bengali scripts which highlighted the ancient culture of the community with a new message to embark upon the voyage of learning. The drama was staged in the rural Santhal villages to inspire the youth to learn the Santhali script. He composed folk songs to spread his ideas. This was the beginning of a new trend in the Santhali language and culture.

The All India Santhali Writers' Association has made an attempt to enlist the Santhali writers of the country. The booklet published by the Association reveals that the community has so far produced around 100 Santhali writers most of whom have published their writings after the country's independence. It indicates that the Santhals did not see the light of education during the British regime. Consequently literacy among the Santhals is at a very low level, and there are only a few readers of the Santhali literature even now. The Santhali writers do not get much patronage from readers. Their books also do not find place in the school and government libraries because of obvious reasons which is another handicap for the Santhali writers.

As a result the Santhals are yet to reach the take-off stage in education. In general education they are far behind the other non-tribal communities. Nevertheless, there is an upsurge among the younger generation of the community to close the gap that exists between the Santhali literature and the other Indian literature.

The Santhali language which happens to be the mother tongue of not only the Santhals, but also Mahali, Birhors and some minority communities who live in the Santhal dominated areas, has been neglected and discriminated by both Central and State Government. So far, many Indian languages, which are spoken by people numbering less than the Santhali-speaking people have received the patronage of the government. Language Akademies have been constituted for such languages by many State Governments to promote these languages. But alas! the Santhali is always relegated to the backyard. In the year 1992 the Central Government included Konkani, Manipuri and Gurkhali which are the mother tongues of some small number of people, in the 8th Schedule of the Constitution of India by an Act of Parliament. But, the Santhali language, despite volumes of Memoranda to the then Prime Minister for its inclusion in the language Bill, could find no place. A single act of kindness of the Government of India by including the Santhali language in the 8th Schedule of the Constitution would have been sufficient to kindle the spirit of learning in the minds of more than 60 lakh Santhali-speaking people of the country. The Government of India, therefore, should give recognition to the tribal languages which have developed their text books and literature in order that the children of the tribals could prosecute their primary education in their own mother tongue as envisages in Article 350-A of the Constitution.

It is pertinent to mention here about the religious beliefs of the Santhals. The *Sarna* religion which the Santhals profess does not seem to hold any philosophy to inspire the community to rise up, higher in the spiritual fields, towards expanding through and mental perfection. The religion has a great bearing on the cultural life of a community. The religion which does not teach love, compassion, altruism, charity and kindness cannot spread in mankind. According to Dr. S. Radhakrishnan, "If religion is not dynamic and pervasive, if it does not penetrate every form of human life and influence every type of human activity, it is only a veneer and not a reality. If on the other hand, we believe that our faith is widespread and its adherents are conforming their acts to the ideals they profess, then the conclusion is inevitable that the religion is invaluable as a means for the improvement of the individual and society."

The Santhals have no doubt preserved their ancient culture and language but they have tended to remain stagnant, static and obscurantist. They have failed to march with the time. The cobwebs of blind faith, superstitions, degenerated, conservative traditions and customs have retarded the progress of the community in the spheres of social and cultural life. The use of ricebeer in all religious and social functions which is based on superstitions and not on scientific reasonings has become a curse for the Santhals. The writers of Santhali literature, therefore, must look beyond the boundaries of ancient orthodox culture and customs and swim in the high seas of knowledge instead of becoming frogs in the wells. In the modern age of high technology and internet, old order must yield place to new.

## REFERENCES

Archer, W. G., *Tribal Law and Justice.*

Bodding, P. O., *A Santhal Dictionary,* Vol 1.

Murmu, Raghunath, *Hital, a Santhali epic poem.*

Radhakrishnan, S., *Recovery of Faith.*

# 11

# JADUPATA IN THE CONTEXT OF SANTHAL CULTURE

*Nilanjana Das (Saha)*

---

*Jadupata* is a distinct tradition of painting done by a non-tribal artists for Santhals in some areas of Bihar and West Bengal. It is also known as Santhal *pata* for its significance in the cultural heritage of the Santhals. It is associated with the rituals and rites, legends and myths, beliefs and prejudices linked with the lifecycle of the Santhals. The *pata* of *Chakshudana*, for example, enfolds the supernatural concept of life after death. We can also trace the subtle and deliberate assemblages of Hindu themes such as those representing Jagannath as *Maran Buru* or Shiva as *Kherba Thakur*. There are also *jadupatas* depicting *Krishna Lila* — the *gopis* going to Mathura for offering curd to *Maran Buru*.

Although all the *patas* painted by the *Jadupatuas* are *jadupatas*, the term *jadupata* specifically refers to a rectangular *pata* called the *Chakshudana pata*. It is keenly associated with the obsequial beliefs of the Santhals.

Since time immemorial, man has been seeking the intangible. *Chakshudana* plays a special part in the tradition, without which the images that are worshipped are believed to be inert. This is a very small *pata* containing ready portraits of a Santhal man, woman or child without eyeballs which are shown to bereaved relatives saying that the deceased is suffering from blindness in the after-life and would continue to do so, untill they send some articles of domestic use or monetary gifts through the *Jadupatua* himself.

Receiving the gifts he finally performs *Chakshudana* or 'bestowal of eyesight' by painting the iris in the blank eyes of the portrait. For this sort of semi-magical act or *jadu* the *pata* is named *jadupata* or magic painting. The caste name of the painters are derived from this. For such an occasion, the *Jadupatua* keeps with him previously drawn portraits of various characters. At the appropriate moment he simply produces one of them according to the age and sex of the dead one. The characters are almost identical. We find some of the finest images in them like that of the *Jog Manjhi* stooping on his stick or the middle aged Santhal woman or the gay plump boy and so on. Sometimes they draw whatever they expect to get for it on the right corner below the *pata*. It could be a chicken or a bowl or the used umbrella of the deceased.

Here is a translated portion of a *Mora Karam*, sung on the occasion, although not at the same time of enacting *Chakshudana* which presents a picture of a *Jadupatua's* role after death. It is collected from the village Moram of the Santhal Parganas.

> You brought him out of the *chatka* (the outer part of a house) and now he stays at the end of the village. But where will the father's *puruchun* (salvation) take place? ........ Holla, the eldest son, do call in *Jado Baba,* he will guard our house, while we take the father to the river for the ceremonial bathing and thus he will attain salvation..... . In their traditional *Binti* they refer to Tel-Kupi-Burni Ghat. The same ritual is also found in districts Puruliya and Midnapore [now Medinipur].

In this way the *Jadupatua*, the spiritual guide, helps the deceased to be relieved from the earthly bindings and guides him or her to heaven. Through the whole demonstration an utmost secrecy is maintained. Outsiders are forbidden to observe the ceremony.

The *Jadupatuas* generally belong to a lower caste Hindu community, live on mendicancy by showing *patas* accompanied with songs to the Santhal audience — viewers in remote villages of the Santhal Parganas in Bihar and those of Birbhum, Bankura, Puruliya and Medinipur in West Bengal. They stay in Santhal villages and also participate in their major ceremonial occasions, though they maintain their own social and religious practices. Here the Santhals are the patrons and the clients are the *Jadupatuas* who are known as *paitkars*. They do not belong to the intermediary caste between Hindu and Islam, as most of the general *patuas* do. They also deny any relation with the *patuas*, although they bear the surname 'Chitrakar' too. It seems to be a later adoption from the *patuas* of Bengal. The *Jadupatuas* belong to various lineages such as Borhamurhe, Larastan, Hentmuria, Khasphoolia (who have the right to kill the goat for sacrifice) etc. Some of them believe that the *Jadupatuas* are ancestors of the entire *patua* community and they explain this with different kinds of evidence. However, the *Jadupatuas* relate their origin to the myth of the birth of Santhal tribe, inspite of being Hindu by birth.

The story is generally depicted in a *Jonmo pata*. It concerns the legend of creation of the earth and the first man and woman — *Pilcu Haram* and *Pilcu Budhi*. They say that after the death of *Pilcu Haram* and *Pilcu Budhi*, *Maran Buru*, the God had created *Jado Guru* (*Jadupatua*) with the dirt rubbed out of his body. As the world was full of sin, the God conferred on him the responsibility of judging the virtues and vices of mankind. *Jado Guru* performed *Chakshudana* of *Pilcu Haram* and *Pilcu Budhi* and bade them farewell to heaven. The seven boys of *Pilcu Haram* and *Pilcu Budhi* then presented them plates, cups, small pitchers and clothes. The eight daughters gifted a cow and bade them goodbye with much pleasure. Besides these they gave them a five-cubid-long cloth as mentioned in the following translation of a song :

*"Ltarcetan Khonjadob Dae Nae Daraekan*
*Jadob Dae Na Bo Cok'Dane,*
*Baro Gun More Moka Cadorte*
*Jadob Dae Na Bo Cok Dane-A"*

["The *Jado Guru* comes from the
*Cetan Desom*, or the land of uncaven earth.
We shall offer him as *Codan*,
a sheet of cloth which is *Baro Hat*".]

Besides the *Chakshudana pata* they also paint and exhibit the scroll type *patas* which are a common type painted by the general *patuas* too. The scrolls contain successively drawn pictures arranged in a vertical order, each of them often decorated with picture frames of a separate designs, patterns, and indicate different episodes. The *Jadupatua* unfolds the scroll gradually as the story is chanted with songs in Santhali which they compose themselves.

At both ends of the *pata* two bamboo sticks are attached. The *Jadupatua* holds the upper stick with the left hand while pointing the episode with the right hand. Then he rolls up the portion of the scroll depicting episodes that have already been narrated on the upper stick and uncovers the next ones. In this way, he narrates the story of the first man and woman, festivals like *Baha* and *Shikar*, the punishments and rewards to the sinners and virtuous people respectively given by *Yama*, the legends of Lord Krishna or the Goddess Kali, and some other themes connected with Hindu mythology. Now we will discuss some of the *jadupatas* which mirror the cultural life of the Santhals to a greater extent featuring the concepts ad supernatural beliefs, myths and fables, historical facts, etc.

We have already discussed the most significant type, the *Chakshudana pata* in the introductory part. The next in importance is *Jonmopata*, which they also call *Karam Binti pata*. Excluding this, two more kinds are found in the Santhal Parganas: (i) *Chatiar Karam*, which consists of almost the same theme, but is a little shorter and it ends with the naming episode of the 12 lineages of the Santhals; and (ii) *Mora Karam,* which is exhibited at the time of obsequies, yet have not been found in any illustrated *pata* excepting some songs. An example of this has been given in the former part.

*Jonmo*, or *Karam Binti* is the longest of all the *patas*, sometimes 15 to 16 feet. Each panel is executed with excellent skill.

The first panel of the *pata* usually represents three prime gods, followed by the dark Universe submerged in water which is drawn in a symbolic, geometric form, the descent of *Thakur* from heaven with the help of the eternal thread, *tore sutam*, the creation of the two birds, *Has* and *Hasil* (swans) and then the vain trials of raising the earth from water by the aquatic creatures like tortoise and prawn and the success of the earthworm, the birth of the earth with *Sirom, Korom* and other plants on her. Next comes the birth of first man and woman — *Pilcu Haram* and *Pilcu Budhi* — from eggs laid by the two birds, the wrath of the fire god, whom they call *Brahma muni*, and the protection provided by *Maran Buru* to the newborns in a stone-house; gradually the discovery of *handi;* the birth of 15 children; afterwards the parent's separation and finally the marriage of the brothers and sisters and thus the distribution of 12 lineages; death of the parents and creation of *Jado Guru*. Some also add other stories like the tale of *Chil Bindha Kanra Gunja Hansdak* or the quarrel between the *Kisku* and *Marndi*. They even depict some later events, such as the battle of "Cae-Campa" etc. The *pata* ends with *Maran Buru*.

There is an interesting tale about the creation of the Great Bear, the group of seven stars which the Santhals call *Budhi parkom*, depicted in a *Chatiar Karam pata*. It is said that before dying, *Pilcu Budhi* had instructed her sons that she should be buried in a place where there is no anguish or suffering and vice but overpowering tranquility. Following her wish, the seven sons, carrying the mother on a bamboo cot, searched for such a place but could not find it on the earth. At last, they all ascended to heaven and then turned into a group of stars and formed the *Budhi parkom* which means the cot of the old woman.

The next important subject is *Baha* or the flower festival, which is observed in the month of *Phalguna* or the spring. It is perhaps the delightful mood of this great occasion when inspired the *Jadupatuas* to choose the theme of painting. It is specially to pay homage to the Sal tree or the *Sari Sarjom* which symbolizes the truth. For the Santhals the Sal is a sacred tree, so, they do not eat the flowers, decorate its flowers in the hair till the ceremony is observed.

The *pata* starts with the glorifying of three gods, *Maran Buru*, whom they very often call *Jagannath*; *Sin bonga* or the Sun god; and *Jaher era*, the goddess of the *jaherthan*. *Jaher* is the holy grove where a Sal tree is planted. Occasionally, they represent the Goddess, *Gosai-era* too. Generally a *Mahua* tree is planted in *jaher* which stands for her. Some also paint *Moreko-Turuiko* or the spirit of the five-six. These tree deities resemble the holy trinity of the Orissan temples—*Jagannath, Balarama* and *Subhadra*. The *Jadupatuas* seem to have cast these alien forms in the cultural milieu and made them fully acceptable to the Santhal viewers by naming them *Maran Buru* and *Sin bonga*.

Next, a fight between a man like monkey or the *Hanru bonga* and *Garuda*, the bird vehicle of Lord Vishnu, is depicted. *Brahma muni*, the god of the Hindu Puranas, is also traced with the three heads whom they name *Sengel muni*. The next panel depicts the ceremonial worship in *jaher* by the priest or (*Naeke*) followed by the associated rituals, festivity and amusements of girls, dancing accompanied with the witty boys clapping hands. The cooking and serving events of the villagers which is the most amusing part of the song composed with their utmost poetic imagination includes quarrels for unequal distribution of food or the mimicking of the activities of the villagers of different nature and temperament. In the middle of the scroll a large, blossomed Sal Tree is represented with men plucking flowers. Sometimes the event of sacrificing a cow is illustrated which recalls an older custom. The scroll invariably ends with the killing of a big *jambro* or the rattle-snake. An overall tendency for detail is noticed specially in the portraits or in some peculiar gestures. The animated figures in remarkable colours and sweeping, vigorous lines make the whole depiction brilliant and dynamic. The songs too are marked by exceptional rhythm and music in companion with others.

*Shikar* or hunting is a favourite occasion of the Santhals which starts on the last day of the festival of *Sohrae* and ends on the *Buddha Purnima*. The theme is generally depicted in a *Ghora* or *Shikar pata*. Each decorated panel represents different groups of hunters with arrows and bows, sometimes followed by a chained hunting dog. Some of them carry a killed prey such as a stag or another animal on the way to home. The *Sorens* who are soldiers, are seen in long strides with guns. The king of the Pargana, the ruler of a few villages attired in a extravagantly bright or showy apparel with a big turban on the head, rides on a horse or giant elephant. There are also rows of many wild beasts like tigers or leopards, deers, etc. Most of the *patas* contain a tiger god or *baghut bonga*, who, according to the belief of the Santhals, protects the hunter from wild animals or other dangers in a forest. The God riding a monstrous leopard holds a whip in one hand. The *Jadupatua* represents him in a violent distortion and grotesque manner which evokes only fear. The form resembles the *Ghazi* of a *Ghazir pata* of the Sunderban area. Though the concept is the same, there are some prominent distinctions between the two. The *Ghazi* appears as a Muslim man with a beard and cap, holding a scripture in one hand and a rosary in the other, the tiger is a Royal Bengal Tiger whereas *Baghut bonga* is featured rather like a Santhal man with a turban on the head and without beard. They draw a stretched-out eye of the tiger, which too is a significant characteristic of the Jain miniature paintings of the 14th century.

There is another kind of *jadupata* which is also extensively practised and performed by the general *patuas,* although their's is a completely different style. This is *Yama pata*. Briefly, the theme which enfolds the Hindu concept of life after death has been introduced by the *Jadupatuas* later. *Yama pata* depicts terrifying punishments given by *Yama*, the Lord of Death, who often is called *Maran Buru.* The God and his associates punish the sinners in accordance with the good or evil work done by them in the previous life on the earth. The sinner is compelled to sit on a nailed wooden seat at Yamapuri and so on. The scroll always ends with the virtuous men enjoying heavenly life. They illustrate *Yama* often with beastly features, perhaps to enhance the terror of the dreadful punishments. The characters are noticeably Santhal in every respect. In this way of showing a *Yama pata*, the *Jadupatua* gives a kind of lesson to the villagefolk to lead a simple and virtuous life and gain a peaceful life in heaven.

Thus we see how the *Jadupatua* ensures his place among the Santhals by exploiting and entertaining them at the same time.

As a spiritual guide he makes the soul free and prepares for the eternal journey to heaven by the act of *Chakshudana* or warns them to abstain from sinful work for a heavenly life in the other world by showing a *Yama pata*. As an artist he, through the visual interpretation of the social and cultural phenomena of their way of life, enriches a wonderful language of folk art.

# 12

# LIVING IN THE KINGDOM OF *BONGAS*
## The Contingencies of Happy Life

***Sitakant Mahapatra***

Every community feels the need to relate itself and its individuals to the world around. The latter has the visible component of the various aspects of nature and the imagined invisible forces that seem to govern human destiny. The individual, the web of relationships that constitute the community, nature and supernatural forces are thus the sides of an integrative, interactive relationship. A view on the totality of this relationship and their interdependence is the worldview of a community.

If one looks at the scenario from the individual's point of view, each one has to find a mechanism of working out his destiny and find a meaning for his life in conjunction with other aspects of the world he lives in. The family , the group, the clan; the various patterns of living together with other individuals constitute easily the most important aspects determining his life. In a real sense, no man is an island. He is linked to the physical reality surrounding him: the forest, the hills, the rivers, the sky, the birds, the animals, etc. Above all is his belief system — the imagined reality of gods, goddesses and ancestors.

The Santhal has certain basic assumptions regarding life. An unseen God has given man his life which has to run its normal course. Each one has been allotted a given span of years and days. God also ordains a healthy life free from disease and sickness. One has to die in normal course when one grows old. Trees and creepers also die when their normal length of life comes to an end. But what if a young man dies falling from a tree or by drowning in a river or is eaten up by a tiger? Well, that would be abnormal and the result of some evil forces working to frustrate God's design. Sickness, disease and accidents happen both to individuals and sometimes to an entire community. An epidemic may wipe out an entire village. A boat sinks in a turbulent river and many individuals of a village die. All that brings about such abnormal end to human lives, all that causes sickness and disease is against the design of the God whom the Santhals refer to as *Thakur Jiu, Maran Devta*. Both the terms *Thakur Jiu* and *Maran Devta* seem to be acquired from the Hindus. Quite often the Supreme deity is simply called *Thakur* or *Devata* as distinguished from *bonga* which is a generic name for spirits. This Supreme God is comparable to the Kondh tribe's *Darmu* or *Dharam Devata*. The Supreme God in the Santhal pantheon is benevolent, non-interfering and detached. He is the giver of life of an allotted span that should normally run its full course without being afflicted by disease and sickness. Death should come at the end of the given span. The Supreme God resides somewhere beyond the clouds and stars. Sometimes the Santhals identify him with *Sin Chando* or the sun as the sun is the creator of seasons, of day and night and life-giving crops and, therefore, of all life including that of human beings.

The Santhal believes that his ancestors are *bongas* who inhabit a kingdom located somewhere between the sky and the earth. When a man dies, the body is burnt on the funeral pyre and a piece of bone is kept in a new earthen jar which is closed by a lid and is buried in the soil at the outskirts of the village. The bones of all such dead in a village are taken out during *Makar Sankranti* some time in January and consigned to a nearby river. This 'bone-drowning' ceremony, *bhandan* and *nahan,* releases the souls of the dead from the limited village territory setting them free to float around midway between the world of the Santhals and the kingdom of the Supreme deity beyond the clouds. The ancestor *bonga* is called *hapram*. The kingdom of *haprams* contains all those dead ever since man lived and died on this earth. It is an overpopulated kingdom located above the village and in any case not far from it, between the clouds and the earth. The ancestor *bongas* are generally benevolent. If the family forgets them totally, however, and does not offer a share of food during festive occasions, they take offence and may turn malevolent causing damage to the concerned family or the entire village. The *hapram*'s influence is primarily on the family to which he belonged but in a minor key this influence also spreads to the entire village. The *hapram* kingdom is thus the invisible *bonga* territory above and beyond the village.

The largest *bonga* territory is the village itself and its immediate surroundings. Here you have *bongas* everywhere. There is the *Orak bonga* (the spirit in a dwelling house), the *Sima bonga* (the spirit guarding the boundary of the village) and the many *bongas* in the *jaher* or sacred grove at the outskirts of the village such as *Maran Buru* (the Great Mountain), *Jaher era* (the Lady of the Grove or the Earth Mother), the *Pargana bonga* (the spirit of the chief of the region), the *Manjhi haram* (the spirit of the village headman), the *Moreko-Turuiko* (the spirit of the five-six) and the *Gosai era* (the spirit of the sister of the *Jaher era*). Of these the most important is *Maran Buru* who is also referred to as *Lita*. He is supposed to have introduced the Santhals to the 'sacramental' ricebeer (the drink that is first offered to the Supreme deity and only then taken), told them that this drink should be taken only on ceremonial religious occasions and not as a daily habit. He created the clans and sub-clans among them, he taught them agriculture and, finally, sex and marriage regulated by clan taboos. He advised the Santhals how to establish the sacred grove and worship the various *bongas* for good health, good crops and general prosperity. In fact next to the supreme deity, the Santhals give the highest priority to *Maran Buru* and *Jaher era* both of whom are worshipped almost always together.

Outside the village limits you have the *Buru bonga* (the spirit of the mountain) and the *Bir bonga* (the spirit of the forest), who are immensely important to Santhal life and society. The Santhals are engaged primarily in agriculture and part of it is what is locally called *podu*, i.e. slash-and -burn cultivation. Before the onset of the monsoon the hill slopes are cleared of trees and shrubs and burnt away. A mix of different seeds, with varying periods of maturing for harvest is then sown. Thus the hills and the forests not only happen to surround Santhal villages, they are essential to their economic activity.

The *bonga* kingdom is a vast, ubiquitous kingdom and the Santhals have to take account of the presence of these spirits right from the individual dwellings to the sky above. It is a world mostly visible, in and around the village but partly visible in the realms where the ancestors and Supreme God reside.The *bongas* are remembered and taken care of both at the household level and the village level. The *bonga* of each particular sub-clan among the Santhal is remembered and worshipped at the harvest festival by the offering of a pig. On each occasion of drinking ricebeer a little is always offered to *Maran Buru*. At every meal the house *bonga* and the ancestors are offered a small fragment of the meal. In the household if someone falls sick and the priest diagnoses it as due to the wrath of a particular *bonga*, the latter is appeared with a special sacrifice. Thus every individual ,every family virtually lives in the midst of *bongas*. The house *bonga*, the *Pargana bonga*, the ancestors, *Maran Buru* and the sickness-causing *bongas* all of them are ever-present realities.

If the individual and the household has to reckon with *bongas* in everyday living, the community also remembers them on specific occasions . Every stage in the agricultural cycle is an occasion for invoking the appropriate *bonga*. The Santhals perform rituals and offerings are made to him from time to time. The sowing of seeds, the weeding operation, the harvesting – each occasion calls for rituals. The annual hunt, when almost the whole village enters the forest looking both for animals to kill and for appropriate roots and leaves for preparation of medicines, is a special occasion for performing rituals. The *bonga* associated with the cattleshed (*Gola bonga*) is worshipped, by all the villagers who pray for the well-being and long life of the cattle.

The village-level worship is thus linked to the Santhal economy— primitive agriculture, cattle rearing and hunting. The villagers join in clearing hill-slopes and they have to worship the hill and the forest *bongas*. The *bongas* of all the stages of agricultural operations have to be worshipped. And then the *bongas* associated with the cattle-shed and annual hunt. In April comes *Baha*, the festival of flowers. It is the season when the entire forest is in blossom, the Sal and *Mahul* trees in particular. During *Baha* the whole village organizes elaborate ritual worship of *Jaher era*, *Maran Buru*, *Ghosai era* and *Moreko – Turuiko*. There is yet another village-level ritual function when the *bonga* for 'first fruits' is worshipped in what is called for *Jantar* (*Jantal*) festival. The entire village also worships collectively whenever there is an epidemic affecting men or cattle.

From the above it is clear that the worship of the *bongas* is performed both at the household and the village levels. The specific occasions and purposes of these two levels of worship are more or less clearly delimited. The head of the household performs the worship at the family level and the Santhal priest at the village level. A birth or a death leads to the pollution not only of the members of the family but also of the *bongas*. The purificatory rite applies equally to the human beings and the *bongas*.

From the above it is clear that the Santhal worldview adopts an integrated perspective of the social , natural and supernatural orders. Man in society has to be blessed by the supernatural *bongas* (including ancestors) who function in and through nature and also as invisibile forces. This organic balance between the natural and the supernatural, between the physical and the moral informs the Santhal worldview.

Rev. L.O. Skrefsrud documented the traditions and institutions of the Santhals in1887 taking down verbatim the sayings of a noted Santhal spiritualist named Kolean. He had clearly noticed an intimate belief in the supernatural order of spirits or *bongas*.This text *Horkoren Mare Hapramke Reak Katha* (Traditions and Institutions of the Santals), later edited by Rev.P.O. Bodding , describes in elaborate details the various *bongas*, the nature of worship in the sacred grove, and spirit-possession. Rev. P.O. Bodding also supplemented this work by his 1928 publication, *The Santals and Diseases* (Memoirs of the Asiatic Society of Bengal) in which he linked the Santhal worldview concerning the spirits and *bongas* to sickness, disease, exorcism and traditional Santhal medicine. Pandit Raghunath Murmu, whom Jayapal Singh called "Guru gomke" or the great spiritual leader, brought together all the invocation songs that accompany different rituals. These were published together as *Bhakhen* in Santhali language and in the Ol Chiki script which he had invented in the 1930s. In *Hital* which is unpublished so far, Murmu described in minute detail the role of *Maran Buru* in the Santhal's quest for health, community solidarity and happiness. There is a remarkable continuity between the 1887 works of Rev. Skrefsrud and the 1969 work of Pandit Murmu as regards *bongas*, ritual worship and invocations. This author had the opportunity of doing a comprehensive documentation of the invocation songs during 1975-77 as a Homi Bhabha Fellow in Orissa and Bihar. The findings marginally differed only from Murmu's compilation.

Given below are samples from some of the invocation songs (altogether there are only 16 such songs or *Bakhens*).

i) We now use these new flowers and fruits
Let there be no disease or sickness from them
Let no disease and pestilence enter our village.
(*Baha* or Flower Festival)

ii) For every seed we sow let there be twelve
And let no disease attack them
Do not allow grass and weeds to grow among them.
Bring plenty of rain-bearing clouds.
(Sowing Festival or *Erok*)

iii) Let there be no disease in our
houses and cattlesheds
let our cattle sheds be full of cattle
Let a crore of animals grow out of one.
(Worship of *Gola Bonga* at *Sohrae* or Cattleshed Festival)

More than a century has passed, since 1887 when Rev. Skrefsrud documented Santhal belief systems. Despite modernization, economic development and the spread of education, the Santhals believe in the existence of multiple three-tiered *bongas* of varying importance and attributes who need to be propitiated with appropriate prayers and offerings of ritual objects so that their blessings are available to Santhal society and enable men and women to live in health , happiness and prosperity.

## REFERENCES

Bodding, P.O., 1928, *The Santals and Diseases,* (Memoirs of Asiatic Society of Bengal), Calcutta

Mahapatra, S.K., 1979, *Bakhen : Ritual invocation song of a Primitive community,* New Delhi : Prachi Prakasan,

____________, 1986, *Modernisation and Ritual Identity and Change in Santal Society,* Calcutta, Oxford University Press.

Murmu, Raghunath, 1969, *Bakhen* (in Ol Chiki script). Orissa : Adivasi, Socio-Educational and Cultural Association.

____________, *Hital,* Unpublished manuscript in Ol Chiki script.

Skrefsrud, L.O., 1887, *Horkoren Mare Hapramke Reak Katha,* Republished (1942). Oslo, Norway, *Ethnografiske Museum Bulletin 6.*

# 13

# SANTHAL WORLDVIEW
## Mixing of Pleasure and Pain

*P. C. Hembram*

Santhals are peace-loving sons of the soil of India. They are a pre-Dravidian and pre-Aryan community and are the descendants of the great heroes of India like Baba Tilka Majli, Sidu, Kanu, Chand Bhairab and others who gallantly fought the mighty British rulers to free themselves of the shackles of exploitation, tyranny, deprivation and oppression. Santhals identify and introduce themselves as *hor* (human beings). They are the largest linguistic, traditional and cultural community in India and possibly in the world.

According to various sources, their total population is a little over 60 lakhs. The districts having a significant Santhal population are :Dhanbad, Dumka, Giridih, Godda, Hazaribag, Katihar, Kodarma, Paschim, Singbhum, Purbi Singbhum, Purnia and Sahibganj in Bihar; Balasore, Bhadrak, Cuttack, Dhenkanal, Keonjhar, Khurda, Mayurbhanj and Sundargarh in Orissa; and Bankura, Barddhaman, Birbhum, West Dinajpur, Jalpaiguri, Maldah, Medinipur and Purulia in West Bengal. Besides, Santhals are also found in the States of Assam, Tripura and across the border in Bangladesh and Nepal. Their population is about 2 lakhs in Assam, more than 22 lakhs in Bihar, about 8 lakhs in Orissa, 2,500 in Tripura and about 28 lakh in West Bengal. Literacy among the

Santhals is low and varies from state to state. The distribution of population in different districts is given in the Annexure. The Santhals, wherever they are, whether in India or abroad, speak a common language called Santhali and uphold their socio-cultural system. They have their own script, Ol Chiki.

Let us understand their worldview. Literally, worldview refers to the perspective with which a man views the world around him during his lifetime and after death. As life is truth so is death. This truth revolves around man. His march from birth to boyhood, adulthood and old age — the stage of infirmity is a long one. He crosses many other stages in the course of his journey and ultimately dies. These stages of life are full of agony, pain and also pleasure. According to them, however, the phase of suffering and pain is more acute than that of pleasures of life which remains suppressed and curtailed. In Santhali this is expressed as, *"Dhaker para dukh"* and *"Dumur para sukh"*. This implies that both pleasure and pain are true and that their peaceful state of life is temporary. It suffers every now and then, by both human acts and natural causes. The incidents that bring misery to their life are not one-day events and happenings. This has been there ever since the birth of human life. When first male and first female children were born there was no soil and no land. Santhals believe that they have been directly begotten by divine birds *Has* and *Hasil*. These birds have been made by *Thakran*, the heavenly mother, consort of *Thakur* from her collar grime. Another belief is that *Has-Hasil* were created by *Lita* from *Sirom Gele*, a herb considered auspicious in Santhal society. *Thakur* gave them life and then they made way to *Jalapuri*, the soil submerged under water. When they got tired, the two of them rested on a lotus leaf. There were *rokage, gongha* (small snail, large snail) and other small and big aquatic animals. *Hasil* laid two eggs on the lotus leaf. In due course of time two children were born from the eggs.The lotus leaf was not strong enough to bear the weight of human children and it ultimately became unstable and not able to float on the waters. The two birds put the children on their backs and flew away. With passing of time the children grew and the birds cried for help so that the human children could be saved.

This agony continued for *gelbar sarne* i.e, 12 years. Let us see how Santhals describe this situation :

*Hai Hai Jalapuri Re*
*Hai Hai Manmi Janamlen*
*Hai Hai Poyrani Sakam C'etan*
*Hai Hai Poyrani Sakam Ho Udul-dubul*
*Hai Hai C'eldo Menai Te*
*Hai Hai Nukin Manowa*
*Hai Hai Okareng Doho Kin*
*Hai Hai Manmi Hopon Jalapuri Re*
*Hai Hai Manmi Hopon Okareng Doho Kin*

What a tragedy! The human children are born on the lotus leaf on water. There is no soil, no land, they are on the back of *Has-Hasil* in the sky. They are crying to alight on land . But alas! There is no land.

*Lita* heard their cry. On reaching the Council of *Devalo* (heavenly settlers), he told them that *Has-Hasil* were flying in the sky with human children on their back. They needed a place to get down where they could take rest. Then everyone in the *Devalo* Council requested *Lita* to find a solution. *Lita* told them:

*"Un Re Aado Litai Menet Thouba Benaou Takin*
*Tobe Reto Nukin Rena Dukdo Chaba Takin;*

*Ot Benaov E-Porton Ena Lita Turighuri*
*Aago Kowai Patal Khon Aach Ren Ko Juri".*

[*Lita* suggests, let us make a place
Then only their sorrows may end;
In hurry *Lita* decides to surface earth on water,
with the help of his associates from *patal* (under the ground).]

He summoned all the aquatic animals like *Icha Raj* (king of lobsters), *Katom Raj* (king of crabs), *Tayan Raj* (king of crocodiles),

*Bower Raj* (king of fishes). They failed to lift the earth from under the waters. Then *Lita* summoned *Kichua Raj* (king of earthworms) and *Hora Raj* (king of tortoises). On the back of a tortoise they placed the divine golden disc and his four legs were tied with a golden chain so that it would not move and disturb the soil.

The earthworm stretched himself from the surface of water to the bottom land under the sea. He held the soil with his mouth at the bottom of water and excreted it through the tail on the golden disc balanced by the tortoise. The soil did not get washed away and in this way the land was surfaced on water. Thus, *Lita* was able to recreate earth. This ended the trouble of *Has-Hasil* forever. They alighted on it for the safe life of human children. Their long march of life begins with suffering and insecurity.

Gradually, the many odds were overcome. In search of secure and peaceful life, the Santhals moved from place to place as Lepec Terel, Peter Bare, Ere Atna, Khodematom, Khojkhaman, Sasang Beda and at last Sari-Sari-Jom-a-disom. This is also called *Jaher disom* or *Sing disom.* The region is full of rivers, water fountains, abundant flowering and fruit plants and many types of grass. Birds play around and chirp in the trees. The area is attractive and suitable for settlement. They lived there happily for 12 years. Thus their long journey came to an end. They were delighted and spoke about the region as *Cae-champa*, the land of flowers, i.e. blissful or prosperous area. As the Santhals ended their sorrow of uncertain conditions, the area is called the land of light and happiness. Also, the area is called *Jaher Disom.* The term *jaher* has been derived from *ja* and *er*. The word in their language means a sacred place (*jahare*) where seed (*ja* or *jo*) can be sown and broadcast (*er*). It signifies a fertile area, so they call their place of worship *jaher* and the bird *sim* (fowl).

At *jaher*, *Sari-sari-jom* (very important plants) are clustered round. *Sari-sari-jom* symbolizes productive soil. Literally , *sari* means truth, *sar* means weapon, *Jom*(a) means food product. Here truth means, simple knowledge derived from the facts and everyday life which provide energy and capacity to save life. So *Sar* or *Aa-sar* (arrow or bow and arrow) is associated with the community since the beginning of the search for a permanent settlement.

Thus they consider the presence of a tree (*Sarjom*), a bird (*sim*) and foodgrain (*iṛi-erba*) in a forest area as a good sign.These symbols act as guidelines to select a place or a location for settlement.

Again, they invoke the possessed spirit to re-ascertain the truth, i.e. existence of *jaher*. The spirit ascertained :

*"Ish-Sa-ha (hus-sa-ha)*
*Ab nam benja*
*Narka nam Jete*
*Hutum nam boda (bode)*
*Gochok in Sakowa*
*Ish-sa-ha"*

[Power is wealth,
It removes difficulties,
It clears the vision,
It leads a man to permanent happiness
And settles him with pleasure
for long long generation.
Power is blessing
That showers happiness and security.]

Let us see the names of the places as mentioned in the Santhali narration with reference to geographical locations. *Sasang beda*, as per the narration , is a very important place where they are divided into 12 sects. *Sasang beda* means, Yellow River Basin. *Gada-beda* means River-bed. Hawang Ho river of China is called Yellow River. *Hawang* means yellow. On the river bank the great Chinese civilization originated. *Giru nai* is another popular name often heared in the *Dansai* song :

*"Hai re hai re*
*Guru ho timin sagin re*
*Guru ho giru nai do,*
*Guru ho timin saging re*
*Guru ho Sura nai do,*
*Iding mese guru ho iding me-se*

*Iding mese guru ho giru nai do*
*Setering mese guru ho sura nai do"*

[Oh preceptor! how far is the Red river,
How far is the Sind river.
Take me to the Red river,
Take me to the Sind river.]

Yuan Rouge river of Indo-China is called the Red river possibly because during migration, ancient Santhals spread over to China and the Indo-China region. Thereafter, they moved through the riverain and reached the north-western part of India, Sind and Punjab, and extended up to Afghanistan, Persia before the arrival of the Aryans.

The name of the place 'Champs' was derived from the *Champa* tree ('champaka', *Michelia champaka*) which bears highly fragrant blossoms and still grows in the neighbourhood as well as in the town itself. The version of the origin of the name finds support from certain inscriptions in which the name *Champaka* is found. In the Santhal tradition, *Champa* is called *"Eae nai disom champa."* Around the place seven rivers flowed far and near. The name is generally uttered with dual expressions as *cae-champa*. It is relevant to mention a popular Santhali song about *cae-champa*.

*"Chae Gar Champ Gar Lili Bichi,*
*Badli, Koyda Likhon Garon.*
*Dayage Chae Champa*
*Badoli Koyda,*
*Dayage Garbon Bagiyat Do."*

(The *cae-champa* is beautifully gardened and is surrounded by leafy green trees. *Badoli Koyda* are highly decorative. With pain in mind, we have left those places.)

Possibly Mandi State has a certain relation with Santhal-Mandi as one of the 12 *paris* (sects or clans). According to Santhal tradition, Mandi is called *kisar* or rich clan group. Also, they are called successful traders.

There is a tale about the origin of Mandi State which takes its name from a remote ancestor of the ruling family. The place was a centre of trade on the main route from Yarkhand and Radok to Hoshiarpur in the plains. This is the bank of the Beas. The place is undulating. The river flows through many hilly terrains resulting in a stiff highland. A portion of the stiff highland is called *dirang*. This term is similar to *darang*. Here *dirang* has come into being after the Beas forced its way through it and again rose into the highland of Suket. This range is well-wooded and fertile and abounds in game. It also contains the famous salt mines. The salt range in Santhali is popularly described as *Lubung Buru* or *Bulung Buru*. But in a song it is uttered as *Lugu Buru*. The range has a reputation of the supernatural powers and tantric cult.
The description is also found in a Santhali song :

*Akoy Guru Ma Darai Kana*
*Lugu Buru Cetante*
*Ghanta Bore Saket Latarte*
*Dharam Guru....Kamru Guru*

[Who the preceptors are!
Walking over the Lugu Hill,
On the side of Ghanta Hill
On the ridges of Saket River.
They are preceptors, Dhonom.....Kamru
(All the twelve gurus come)
Walking over Lugu Hill
Down ridges of Saket]

All the hills, the forests, the river-beds and the surroundings are believed to be the abodes of supernatural powers. All the 12 gurus, according to Santhal tradition, extended their blessings to the community for their safe and happy life.

The life, the creation itself is the gift of godly powers. So, they find gods all around : *otre, re, dare-sakam nari re, da-rimil, samani re bong dare do charao hena aa*. The Santhals believe that in soil, stone, plant-leaf and creepers, in water, clouds and sky, everywhere the benevolent power exists.

Gods may get angry if man does not follow the rules of nature. A tree should not be cut in the night; one should not throw stones towards a tree when it is taking rest, i.e. night time . Nobody should set out to hunt at night or kill a bird at night when it is asleep. One should not urinate here and there, nor pass excreta, because such places are marked for God who takes rest or shelter there. He would get angry.

A natural situation should not disturbed since nature blesses man if he acts righteously. Once a place is confirmed suitable through divination, they organize *jaher* and plan the settlement. *Jaher* area is always fertile, as such it is good for livelihood. In Santhali, a new settlement is called *di* or *dihi*, when *di* satisfies all the components of organized social conditions it is termed *ato* or *atu*. Literally *ato* means village and *atu* stands for sources of water that may flood the settlement. The life conditions are self-sufficient in the village . The council of families living in the village is called *ato-more hore* or *ato more ko*. The members of the village council are *Majhi, Jog Manjhi, Godet, Paranik* and other members of the village.

Bow and arrow (*aa-sar*) is considered a vital weapon in the community . The weapon is never touched by foot and if it happens by mistake one has to bow one's head before it in veneration. In the earlier days the umbilical cord of a new born baby was cut with the sharp edge of an arrow-head and the same arrow was placed vertically on the head side of the baby. The bow and arrow provides a sense of security. People carrying the weapon move safely without any fear including that accruing from evil forces. This is the divinated weapon used by *Moreko* — the great force of village establishment. The *sar* also symbolizes manly power.

Similarly *nahel garke* is the symbol of sanctity and community solidarity. *Nahel* literally means plough — the source of agricultural activities. Here it stands for the whole community and village economy. This economy revolves around the *nahel*. It is a sacred instrument and is always kept with a sense of reverence. *Garke* means the placement which actually refers to the effect of the mandates to all villagers and social conditions. The term has now come to mean obligation to social rules. The violation of it is believed to bring destruction and social disaster.

This further symbolizes social solidarity controlled and guided by the village council, i.e. *Moreko*. So, this is the narration in the community:

*More koko siyo kana*
*Lugu Buru sotalre*
*Ghanta bare hana sahare*

(The five members are ploughing the terrace land of *Lugu Buru* on the other side of *Ghanta bare*.)

There is again a very popular saying specially by children : when the climate is bad, the clouds hover in the sky and bring heavy showers. The children pray that rough weather vanishes quietly and pleasant sunshine appears.

*Do Da Chala Me*
*Lugu Buru Te*
*Dela Situng Hiju Me*
*Ganta Bari Te.*

(Bad weather and clouds should vanish to *Lugu Buru* and pleasant sunshine appear in the thickly planted area.)

*Ghanta bare* is a good network of villages with thick plants and shades where even sunshine cannot enter. The children pray that sunshine should come to *Ghanta bare* instead of *Lugu Buru* which does not have plants and is sparsely planted and so rain should go there.

It has already been mentioned that the Santhals believe that there are gods everywhere. They call their settlement *bonga disom*. *Bonga* means heavenly spirits who located *bir disom* and erected *atore pairi* (village settlement). A *Baha* song runs as follows :

*Akoy Mai Chiyaiya Ho Bit Disom Do*
*Akoy Mai Chiyai - Ya Ho Atore Pairi*
*Marang Buru Chaiyai - Ya Ho Bir Disom Do*
*Jaher era Chiyai-Ya Ho Atore Pairi.*

[Who will locate the forest land
Who will erect village for generation!
*Maran Buru* will locate the forest land
*Jaher era* will erect the village for generation.]

So, the forest land is the gift of *Maran Buru* and village settlement is the creation of *Jaher era*. *Jaher* is also the term for the place of worship of the Santhals. The Mother God in the Santhal pantheon is closely associated with *Maran Buru*. She cannot, however, be understood as his consort in the strict sense. She is merely a companion, a complement of the other. *Thakur* and *Thakran* are above every supernatural embodiment.They are Supreme, and are never worshipped for material gain. *Maran Buru* and *Jaher era* are the guide, teacher, saviour and custodian of the complete Santhal community.

They erected a *jaher* and showered resources for the Santhals. This is evident in the following song :

*Jahera ge Ja gosae dhirighutu Jahere*
*Jahera ge Ja gosae Sari Sarjom Jahera.*
*Akoy medoy Jahera ja gosae dhirikghutu jahera*
*Akoy medoy Jahea ja gosae sarisarjom jahera*
*Marang burui Jahera ja gosae dhirighutu jahera*
*Jaher era jahera ja gosa sri sarjom jahera*
*Moreko ko jahera Jo gosae dhiri ghutu Jahera*
*Turui koko Jahera ja gosae Sari sajom Jahera.*

[Who erected *jaher* around laterite soil,
Who turned it into a place of all resources!
*Maran Buru* erected *jaher* around laterite soil,
*Jaher-era* turned it into a place full of resources
*Moreko* enliven a *jaher* amidst stony land

*Turuiko* took care to make it a green place.]

A *jaher* is seen in a place full of pebbles, stones or laterite soil. At present a *jaher* is seen to be surrounded by Sal grove. Here *Maran Buru* stands as a source of water who turn the laterite soil into fertile land called as *jo-er* — area or food growing place. Then, *Moreko-Turuiko* who represents the village community lived there for several generations. There are several such narrations scattered here and there that give an idea about the Santhals' life, creation and survival. I like to add some more relevant information which may throw light on the Santhal worldview.

Women in the tribal society enjoy liberty equal to men. *Majhi era* or *Naeke era* is traditionally the leader of womenfolk. She is informed of seasonal changes by other womenfolk of the society. The women speak in their language which has words to express every emotion and meaning of tribal life.They have a very simple way of life with all reverence to their ancestors, deities, surrounding environment and nature. Their main resource is the natural surroundings. It informs, instructs and blesses them. From the following song this becomes clear :

*Hesa ma chotereja gosae Tude doy raa let,*
*Bara ma lare ja gosae qotrot doy saket let,*
*Des chong achuren ja gosae got Tude doy raa let,*
*Disom chong bihuren ja gosae got rot day sahet let,*
*Ajom mese Naike era ja gosae Tude doy rage let,*
*Aten mese boyo ho ja gosae got rot doy sahet let,*
*Des chong achuren ja gosae Tude doy rage let,*
*Disom chong bihuren ja gosae got rot doy, sahet let.*

[On the top of the Pipal tree, the woodpecker is humming,
Under the Banayan branches the *gotrot* is growling,
Oh madam! *Naeke* listen the woodpecker is humming,
Oh madam! *Naeke* pay attention, *gotrot* is growling.
Well, I listened, the woodpecker is humming,
Well, I heard attentively , the *gotrot* is growling,
Yes, every year earth revolves round the completion,

so, the woodspecker is humming,
Certainly, the country's climate has completed the
cycle and *gotrot* is growling.]

The tribal life continues in a simple rhythm. Any problems or difficulties which enter their life are considered a bad omen. They feel aggrieved and sometimes even desert the place.

A Santhal community term their group as *ho* or *hor.* The term 'Santhal' given to them by the outsiders now stands as a constitutional name. At the inter-community level, they use their own term which marks their identity.

The birth of a child in Santhal society is considered as a matter of joy. The child is called *nowa pera* or new guest. He is taken into the society through *Chatiar* ceremony, i.e. process of socialization. The ritual is presided over by *Manjhi.* A Santhal child is not only a member of a particular family but also a member of the village.

Hence, we see that every house of the village is a house of *Manjhi,* the head of the village and chief of the society. Virtually, *Manjhi* is the head of a family so far as social matters like birth , marriage and death of a village family member are concerned. Before concluding the *Chatiar* ceremony the village elders utter, *Babu do sendra re karka re, Daran re domel re khelheperov re soto kai gate kai mesa kai pe; Mai do sahan re sakam re da ghat kuing ghat, Enec re, Sereng re durang re mesa kai seled kai pe.* (Let our boy be allowed and given company in all hunting expeditions, trips, games and competitions; let our girl be given company, guidance, also to be taken with and allowed to go to jungle for collection of leaves, firewood, mushrooms, to collect and fetch water, in all dances, gatherings and merry-making.)

Through marriage, Santhals enter a responsible social life. In the concluding session of the marriage ceremony at the residence of the bride, before the happy send-off of the new couple to the groom's house both the *Manjhis* (belonging to the bride and groom's village) sit together and advise them about their family life as :

*Ma tehendo kasmar totkole tol aat bina*
*Ekla dukla daran ban gano tabina sedaido*
*Matre ghatre horre birre monkusi bin dara*
*Leda teheng khon do pouri pourijanga gidi*
*Hoyo tabina, babu sendram seno karkam seno*
*Aa jahagem halang aa tumal aa adha do agui me*
*Adha jomme, mai am ho da ghat pukri ghat*
*Ekla dukla alom seno aa; natya era, hanhar*
*Era, se erel kuri sao seno me, jaha gem daka*
*Utui adha do jawai lagit sarech daho ka me.*
*Teheng khon do mit mone mit jiou hor ena bin,*
*Eper hedec, kaija khapari re, majhi henai, ato*
*More hor then ardas bin*

[Today both of you are tied with *kasmar totko* — a wooden bell which means that a social responsibility has been conferred upon you. Now you are forbidden to enjoy free and independent life. Before your marriage you have enjoyed free life without any botheration. Henceforth you have to walk together step-upon-step. Young man! when you go for hunting and get something edible, eat half of it and bring the other half for your wife. Young lady you too! henceforth do not go alone to jungle, ponds. Always go with your mother-in-law and sister-in-law. Whatever you cook, keep the share of your husband. Whenever there are any differences, quarrels and other problems, tell your elders, *Manjhi* and other members of the village council.]

Thus we see that the parents of bride and bridegroom are not the decisive authority to recognize or establish their identity — where, how and what way they will be placed in the family and in the society. The institution of marriage is a fundamental part of social life. It marks the beginning of family. This gets reflected in the following song :

*Dong Do Okaredo Janam Len*
*Dong Do Okaredo Busar Len*

*Dong Do Dong Lasai - Lasai;*
*Dong Do Hihire Janam Len*
*Dong Do Pipiri Re Busar Len*
*Dong Do Dong Lisai - Lisai*

[Where marriage first occurred
Where marriage first took place
Marriage is grand and beautiful
Marriage first occurred at *Hihiri*
Marriage first took place at *Pipiri*
Marriage is beautiful and grand.]

*Hihire* and *Pipiri* is the cradle of human origin. *Pilcu Haram* and *Pilcu Budhi* — first progenitors of Santhal community, coupled there. The place is called the 'eternal locality of human generation'. Religion in Santhali is understood by the term *dhorom*. They say,

*Abodo Hor, Abona, Saota Hena Aa Ror Hena Aa,*
*Ol Hena Aa, Dhorom Henatabona, Ona Khatir*
*Abobon Bonga Buru Aa.*

[We are human beings, we have society,
we have language and means of writing, we have religion.
For that we worship.]

Santhals speak of *bonga buru* to mean the worshipping of gods and goddesses. Literally, *bonga* means a god and *buru* means hills. They say gods and goddesses ordinarily dwell in the hills, or gods and goddesses are as big as the Himalayas and powerful. It again throws light on their relation with nature.

In Santhal society, there are twelve clans referred to as *paris* : *Hansdak, Murmu, Kisku, Hembram, Marndi, Soren, Tudu, Baske, Beska, Dhodka, Paurie* and *Chore*. Out of these, *Chore, Dhodka* and *Pauria* do not exist anymore. It is believed that due to an attitude of separatism and adoption of practices forbidden among the people, the three clans have been effaced from Santhal society. These *paris* in the later phase perhaps mingled with the remaining nine and became one with them. There is a unique characteristic of the Santhal community — rich and poor, lord and peasant, wise and laymen — all enjoy equal rights and privileges in the society. Economic disparity never affects the solidarity of the community.

The Santhals are not idolators. They worship the *Bonga buru*. *Bonga* (spirits) have free form. So they do not like to personify and limit them. They worship in the open place at *jaher*. But they prepare *khond*, the mundane boundary for the particular deity for worship.*

'God' and *johar* express solemn vows. Literally, 'God' means, bowing down one's head to superiors, to *bongas*, as a mark of respect to social norms and mandates of the society. While worshiping 'God', the folded hands of a man or a woman also touch the earth. *Johar* means respectful prayer to *bongas*. This also expresses a wish of happiness, victory for seniors and members of same age group. Santhals wish each other saying *johar* when they first meet.

Whenever they meet, they talk about the sorrows and sufferings. According to them, human birth is a great gift (in their tongue they say, "*manmi jonom do adu dular jonom*"). A similar saying is, "*dhuri-dharti re soto sumung jiou are mit bita lac lagit abodoban namal ghatalo kana, kaija khapari kana, mapa gopoc' kana, ikhan hasarena hormo hasarege mohor meta aa hoyrena jiou hoyre mesa aa*" (the earth is made of dust particles, life is short and even the belly is very small. But desire leads a man to roam from place to place, men quarrel and kill each other. After death, mortal body is mixed with earthly dust and life in the air). As *bonga-buru* the end of life is called *Guju-buru* which leads to eternity, the divine abode. Also it is termed *bonga-en* which means journey to the abode of gods or celestial bodies.

The concept of re-birth is very prominent in the Santhals.

---

* Similar religious practices were evidenced during the Sumerian civilization in Mesopotamia BC 3200-2800. In the beginning there was multiplicity of cults. Gods were represented as animals or as the heads of animals and the solar religion was of great importance. Another important feature was the practice of decoration of the walls with colour plugs of clay in the mosaic fashion which is still evidenced in the Santhal community.

They want to be born again and again which is confirmed in their saying, "*janam ruwar*". This further refers to their faith that the soul is immortal while the body is mortal.

## Conclusion

In this article I have attempted to clarify the worldview of the Santhals. Worldview is the outcome of the socio-cultural situation of a community. It includes the different life conditions, stages and values of each phase having a long-term appeal in human society. I have also explained the situation as mentioned in their *Binti* from the birth as human beings to all the stages thereafter. Besides I have made it a point to highlight some of the results of the practices which have influenced their life to a great extent.

The main socio-religious characteristics of the Santhals are as follows :

1. The society is devoid of caste hierarchy. Santhal is a casteless society.
2. By birth no person, family, clan group is superior or inferior.
3. Image or idol worship is absent and there is no temple in Santhal society.
4. Blood offering is prevalent in the community.
5. Earlier practice of cow sacrifice is greatly restricted.
6. Both burial and cremation are practised. A chicken is dedicated to the dead body.
7. Offering during worship is made within the pictorial boundary known as *khond* as a mark of mundane relationship of the supernatural power.
8. Priesthood is not held by a particular clan group or a sect but it is owned by the family members of the first settlers of a village. Occasionally selection of a successor of the old priest is held if he leaves no issue (male child ) or consanguineous relations. Such a selection is made mainly by a divinated person and it is undisputed.

Worship in the Santhals is called *bonga-buru*. There are two types of *bongas* in the Santhal society : *Manam bonga* and *Jaher bonga* or Universal Gods. *Manam bongas* are local gods. Their names and potential vary from place to place. But *Jaher bonga* or Universal Gods are one and the same in the Santhal pantheon. *Orak bongas* or household deities come under the jurisdiction of *Manam bongas*.

The Santhals refer to truth as *sari*, which means the factual aspect of the universal situation. This is first derived from the attainment of perfection, i.e. organized settlement. From a Santhali song we see :

*Sari-lo-rilo,*
*Ja-gosae kunam ja Taower,*
*Dare dare Jo-en*
*Sakam Sakam Jo-en*
*Sari-lo-rilo.......*
*Ja gosae kunam jo taower.*

[Cheer of truth, oh spirit!
the plants are laden with fruits,
each branch bears fruits,
each leaf covers fruits.
cheers of truth, oh spirit!
the trees are laden with fruits".]

*Sari-lo-rilo* here expresses abundant bearing of fruits by every branch of every tree which has made the trees bend and near to the ground. This symbolizes fertile land on which all kinds of fruit trees and paddy plants grow. Such a place is selected after a long period of search by *Moreko-Turuiko* to organize a *jaher.*

Salvation is not the ultimate aim of Santhal life. They call it *sari-en* meaning attainment of perfection and similarly *bongaen* is a term for the departed soul which shelters in godly abode.

It has been mentioned that the Santhal community is divided into twelve *paris*. Twelve *paris* having twelve numerals, one to twelve is the unique characteristic in the Santhal society and Santhal life. The same form is seen as the universal characteristics and philosophical guidelines of the world because, twelve numerals have great significance as they can turn chain all the time factors of the universe. Nowhere does a numerical form exist in such a unique form to describe a traditional culture and society has been existing and maintaining its traditional culture and language even in the transition period of modernisation when the tribal world is being deformed and is facing extinction and identity crisis in terms of its language and cultural inheritance.

ANNEXURE

## DISTRICT-WISE ANALYSIS OF THE SANTHAL POPULATION

| Sl. No. | Name of State/District | Total Population | Santhal Population | Percent |
|---|---|---|---|---|
| I | Assam | | 2,00,000 | |
| II | Bihar | | | |
| | Deogarh | 933113 | NA | |
| | Dhanbad | 2674651 | 240718 | 9 |
| | Dumka | 1495709 | 568370 | 38 |
| | Giridih | 2225480 | 356077 | 16 |
| | Godda | 861182 | 120565 | 14 |
| | Hazaribag | 1601576 | 64063 | 4 |
| | Katihar | 1825380 | 109522 | 6 |
| | Kodarma | 629264 | 37755 | 6 |
| | Paschim Singhbhum | 1787955 | 178795 | 10 |
| | Purbi Singhbhum | 1613088 | NA | |
| | Purnia | 1878885 | 93944 | 5 |
| | Sahibganj | 736835 | 309471 | 42 |
| III | Orissa | | | |
| | Balasore | 1696583 | 169658 | 10 |
| | Bhadrak | 1105834 | 33175 | 3 |
| | Cuttack | | NA | |
| | Dhenkanal | | NA | |
| | Keonjhar | 1337026 | NA | |
| | Khurda | | NA | |
| | Mayurbhanj | 1884580 | 567282 | 28 |
| IV | Tripura | | *2200 | |
| V | West Bengal | | | |
| | Bankura | 2805065 | 336607 | 12 |
| | Barddhaman | 6050605 | 363036 | 6 |
| | Birbhum | 2555664 | 153340 | 6 |
| | West (N&S) Dinajpur | 1200924 | 180138 | 15 |
| | Jalpaiguri | 2800543 | NA | |
| | Maldah | 2637032 | 184592 | 7 |
| | Medinipur | 8331919 | 1333107 | 16 |
| | Puruliya | 2224577 | 333686 | 15 |

*NA* : Figures not available * As per 1981 Census

*Sources* : 1. The Census Report 1991

2. *The Encyclopaedic District Gazetters of India,* Gyan Publication, New Delhi

REFERENCES

Bodding, Paul Olaf, 1942, *Traditions and Institutions of Santals*, Oslo : D.W. Brogers, Boktrykken.

____________, 1993, *Santhali Dictionary* (Re-published), New Delhi : Gyan Publishing House.

Charak, Sukdev Singh, *History and culture of Himalayan States,* Vol. II, Himachal Pradesh, Part II.

Hembram, P. C., 1988, *Sari-Sarna,* Delhi : Mittal Publications.

Murmu, Ramchand Sadhu, 1979, *"Lita Godet" - Sadhu Ram Chand Murmu Uihar Bathan.* Midnapur, Kamarbandi.

Raiska, Ramdas Tudu, *Kherwal Bongsba Dhorom Puthi,* Ghatsila Singhbhum : B. Chakravarty & Co. Ltd.

# 14

# THE SANTHAL WORLD OF SUPERNATURAL BEINGS

*N. Patnaik*

Of the major tribal groups of India the Santhal is one occupying the third position in the order of numerical preponderance.The two tribal groups at positions above the Santhal are the Bhil and the Gond. These two tribes have each several subgroups. If the total population of each of these two major tribal groups is distributed among their respective subsections then each subsection becomes a minor tribe. Moreover, some of these subsections are so different from their parent tribal groups in language, social organization and culture that they can easily be regarded as separate tribal groups.

The Santhal gives a different picture altogether. It has no subsection and , therefore, no difference in language and culture. In view of this the Santhal may be considered the single largest homogeneous Scheduled Tribe in the country. Their main concentration is in Bihar, West Bengal and Orissa. The name Santhal is given to the tribe probably by the Hindus. Otherwise they call themselves *hor* (man) and are known as *Manjhi* in West Bengal.

The Santhal has an independent language known as Santhali and it is one among the few tribal groups having a well developed script which goes by the name Ol Chiki (written script). Many books have been printed in Ol Chiki.

The Santhal culture is full of folktales, folklores, myths, legends and riddles. These rich oral literature speaks volumes about the creation of the Universe and mankind. One can get very important information about the Santhal customs and traditions, mores and values, sanctions and standards, ethos and worldview from these folktales.

The Santhal was once a wandering tribe. In course of peregrinations they visited many places and travelled from one land to the other. In 1833 the government demarcated an area surrounding the Rajmahal hills and made it a new district which was called Damin -I-Koh. This was where the Santhals finally came and settled down.It was the idea of the government to populate this new district so that there would be substantial increase of revenue and trade. Finding the Santhal hungry for land, their immigration from farther south to this new district was accelerated. They cleared the forest and reclaimed the lands for cultivation.By doing so they became the *khuntkatidars* or original clearers and cultivators of the land. Following the Santhals, flocks of traders and merchants and money-lenders infiltrated into the area and within a few years the rapacious habits of the traders and moneylenders reduced the Santhals to serfs and bonded labourers.

The Santhals love land more than their life. Possession of land which they cultivate was the most powerful motive in Santhal life. A Santhal's land not only provides economic security but is a powerful link with his ancestors. In other words, the land is part and parcel of his spiritual as well as economic heritage.

High rates of interest, attachment of land for debt, repayment by debt or bondage, etc. drove these once contented and happy people to despair. When hard times and bad seasons came, the canker hiding in the bloom of apparent peace and happiness showed itself; they rose, goaded to rebellion in 1856 by the wrongs which they were suffering, and in their struggle to shake off the incubus, the pleasant chimera collapsed and they were reduced to a state of starvation and utter misery. It was at this time that many missionaries landed up in the area, extended their help in whatever way they could, established mission centres to proselitize them and carried out ameliorative measures particularly in the fields of health and education.

One may have the feeling that the Santhals must have undergone a great transformation as a result of their cultural contact with the missionaries and other agents of change. It is, in fact, not so. No motive is so strong among the Santhals as the preservation of the mores, values and other traits of their cultural identity. What Man (1861)has observed in this regard is reproduced below.

> "As my acquaintance with them has been for the most part confined to Sonthalia Proper, which more immediately includes and surrounds the Raj Mahal hills, it is somewhat difficult to state whether a people so greatly increased and multiplied, and spread over such a large tract of country, have kept up intact, in other districts, the same traditions and habits as in Sonthalia, but from a casual interview with an intelligent Sonthal in Midnapore. I discovered his ideas of his race, his religious ceremonies, and all his customs were identical with those mentioned by another of his tribe at Simra, in the Bhaugulpore district : and these two places are some 300 miles apart".

Nowhere do the Santhals now live in isolation as the area inhabited by them is easily accessible and there is direct contact between them and other people. With the spread of outside culture especially the products of its machine technology, the acceptance of the new ways of doing old things was naturally expected, but the Santhals have shown very little change in their business of living. Certainly, there has been some change in the different aspects of their culture, but they appear to be superficial having no force to change their cultural core. As compared with the vast changes wrought in the surrounding Hindu culture the changes marked in the life of the Santhals are very slight.

A review of the life of the Santhal may reveal the factors that militate against change and those favouring cultural stability and conservatism. It may be mentioned that the study of change by itself is meaningless unless it is projected against a base line measured in time and space.

Conservation and change and development are the result of the interplay of the environmental, historical and psychological factors. Besides, they are linked to the enculturative processes. The question to be discussed at this stage is, What kind of vision and conception the Santhals have of everything which they experience or think to have existed around them? and What, according to them, constitutes a good and happy life?

What previous observers have found out corroborates that the pleasure-principle or play-principle seems to actuate them most. All the villagers may spend the whole day running after a bird that hops and fleets from tree to tree being injured by the arrow of a boy. The date for a festival in one village is fixed in a way that it is followed by festivity in adjoining villages so that the people of the region participate in it over an entire fortnight. There appears to be a noticeable obsession with somehow continuing it and not letting it to come to an end. This is not to create an impression that the Santhal is not capable of hard work and that one and all exhibit such a pleasure principle. There are some among them those who are trying to bring about change in this attitude but nobody pays much attention to their words because they are few in number.The reactionaries and reformists among them who have accepted change and innovative ideas are labelled as, 'Not-Santhal'. For the general public in the Santhal society what stimulates them most is the pleasure-principle and what irritates them most is to submit themselves to a time schedule in any work.

The next point for discussion is the Santhal's view of conception of 'good and happy' life. According to them four conditions constitute a happy life. The first and foremost condition which brings happiness is that of well-being and freedom from disease and sickness.They believe that disease and sickness are unnatural and say that human beings have a natural right to health and life and that they ought to live to old age. There are hundreds of *bongas* or evil spirits, as they are called, around them and they harass people and cause disease, illness and death.

The second condition is to be free to enjoy oneself without restrictions of time schedules. This component emphasizes the principle, "to eat, drink and be merry". The most harmful element in the play principle of which many remain unconcerned is conspicuous consumption and expenditure. The obsession for prolongation of expensive rituals such as *Baha* or *Maker* clearly shows that propensity to save and economize the festivities is very low among the Santhals.

The third condition is to have friction-free and balanced relation with all members of the group, in family and in society. The Santhal is an ardent believer in social action which is an integral part of the traditional, social and political organizations. The social actions are determined and decided by the traditional leaders such as *Manjhi, Jɵg Manjhi, Naeke* in whom the people have faith and confidence.

Therefore, all social actions are free from friction, envy and resentment. Such actions on the contrary reinforce the harmony, stability and cohesiveness among the village-folk. In this respect the Santhal excels all other tribal groups. As the traditional leadership which is the guardian of the social customs, ritual practices and belief system is followed by the people and not challenged, both the enforcement of the rules of conduct and adherence to such rules take place in normal course of action without any stress and strain.

The fourth constituent of a happy life is to have a balance between the world of men and the world of spirits. The supernatural world comprises *bongas* of various orders, benevolent spirits of the dead ancestors who continue to have interest in the affairs of their survivors, *bongas* of the sacred grove who wish welfare of the village-folk, and malevolent and mischievous *bongas* who are found in all places in the Universe.

*Maran Buru* gives life to people for a certain period. The Sun God makes day and night and brings rain and gives sunlight. He helps people to get good crops and punishes them too with famine and drought if they infringe the rules of conduct and violate social taboos.

The *bongas* roam about and interfere in the affairs of human beings. There are *bongas* at the outskirts of the village and inside the village boundary. There are forest *bongas*, mountain *bongas*, spring, *bongas*, tree *bongas*, home *bongas*, underground *bongas*, etc. The number of *bongas* is a large organized body. All these *bongas* are regularly propitiated on several occasions as otherwise they would cause havoc. They are believed to be hungry, thirsty, angry and displeased. Therefore, sacrifices are offered to them so that they do not interfere in the health and happiness of the people.

The Santhals believe in witchcraft even in the present day.All untimely deaths and illnesses which do not yield themselves to treatment are attributed to the machinations of witches. Women who are witches are frequently murdered in revenge for deaths which they are supposed to have caused.The Santhal women are obliged to hold meetings at night in which *mantras* and songs are repeated to acquire uncanny powers.

The school of ojhaism is very active in its functions. Divination, oracle and herbal medicines, which the Santhals resort to at the time of illness, are day-to -day affairs throughout the length and breadth of the areas inhabited predominantly by the Santhals. Even today when modern medical practices have been placed within the easy reach of the Santhals, there goes on as much sorcery, magic and witchcraft as was the case years back.

As in the aspects of witchcraft and occultism so in the material culture particularly dress, food and drinking habits, house types, settlement pattern there appears to be least change.The same stability is noticed in dance and music in which there is nothing new.

Close observation of the Santhal society may, however, reveal some minute changes in certain aspects at the individual level.But such changes do not seem to have any effect in obliterating the cultural core and cultural pattern. The mores, sanctions, rules of conduct, wall paintings and colour-washing, neatness of settlement, bodily cleanliness, clan organization, rites of passage, sorcery, witchcraft, curative practices and herbal medicines and what not of the Santhal culture continue to be distinctive of the community. So the question is, What factors have been favourable for the preservation of original cultural traits, richness of folklores and folktales, widely known mythologies and legends, effectiveness of herbs, medicines and indigenous remedies, science of ojhaism and mental therapy, undiminished impact of traditional secular and religious guardians and the fear complex linked with bongaism?

Santhals are ethnocentric to the extreme. They believe that their own way of life is all-important and the best. The ethnocentrism is best illustrated in their myths and folktales. This strong sense of ethnocentrism serves as a very important factor making for intra-tribal integration and cultural stability. What a Santhal is, is best understood by the saying, "A million Santhals have a single word: Whatever the individual he is first and last a Santhal".

The Santhal culture is a hidden treasure in so far as its medicine complex including its constituent elements of ojhaism and bongaism is concerned. This aspect contains valuable and important information most of which is in the memory and put into practice as and when required.Some simple remedies are amazing. The use of leaves of the *Champa* tree, for example, to keep the hair free from lice makes all the expensive shampoos redundant. Out of the realization of importance of documentation of such a valuable aspect of the Santhal cultural heritage by Dr. (Mrs) Kapila Vatsyayan and Prof Baidyanath Saraswati grew a pilot study which afforded access to this treasure.

## II

The main components of a Santhal's worldview are Man, Nature and God and the relationship that exists between these parts. This three dimensional relationship can be represented as a triangle each arm of it representing one of the parts of the worldview. The arms of the triangle may be equilateral in some cases and unequal in others depending upon the emphasis laid by the communities on the different parts of the worldview.

Among the Santhals the people essentially confront the spirit world, (*bonga* world). They have a kind of worldview in which the confrontation of the *bongas* is paramount. Man and nature are only subordinate entities. By nature they mean land, water, woods, etc., as do all other communities. Similarly, the Man whom they call *hor* is on the fringe of their interest and attention.Their whole attention has centred upon the supernatural beings and the rest of the universe appears to them as a hazy hinterland. If we are to represent in a triangle the Man-Nature-God relationship as we find among the Santhals we would draw a triangle in which the supernatural base is by far the longest line of the three.

In order to have a clearer understanding of the cosmology of the Santhals and the place which the spirit world occupies in their cosmos it is necessary to give a picture of the setting in which the Santhals lead their lives. They live mostly in villages. Each household has a house of its own in the village. Of all other tribal communities of India particularly of eastern India none has quite the same taste for neatly arranged buildings, the same setting for tidy spacious living and the same ingenuity and genius for domestic architecture. Although the houses are mud-walled and straw of grass or tile thatched, the finishing of the grey coloured walls and floor excels the cement-like precision. The wall paintings of various floral and geometric designs distinguish the Santhal houses from the dirty, ugly-looking hovels of neighbouring tribals communities.The long and neat village street dominates the scene and the individual houses have each its entrance facing the village street.This settlement pattern and house type is symbolic of the Santhal unity and solidarity.

The immediate surroundings of the village provide land for kitchen garden which is attached to each house at the back and there are fruit trees all around. Maize and millets are grown on the uplands and there are *Mahua* trees in abundance which litter the ground with flowers in the months of March and May. The Santhal women are found early morning bowing down to collect the soft *Mahua* flowers which are used for preparing delicious dishes and for distilling liquor.

Beyond the uplands lie vast stretches of rice fields giving an appearance of a green carpet of paddy plants. Here and there springs flow supplying drinking water to the people. To the Santhals two things are of the greatest value:one, the rice fields which are vital to their life and the other, the forest which is dear to their heart. The nearby forests are visited by the Santhals for various purposes like collection of fuel, leaves, twigs, timber and flowers and collection of roots and tubers, which form the mainstay of the kitchen during a famine. Hunting animals in the forest is the most delightful pursuit and the annual hunt is observed with the greatest gaiety and pleasure.

The Santhal society is characterized by democratic equality. Wealth matters little in their life. The clans are règarded as equal to one another and there is no class distinction either in status or in occupation. The villages are generally multi-clan in composition and each clan has a number of sub-clans.

The Santhal villages are social and political entities with great cohesion and continuity. Each village, has a well-established political organization with a secular head-man called *Manjhi* who is a man of great prestige. He presides over the village meetings when they are held to discuss matters relating to the village.To assist him there are two other functionaries, namely, *Paranik* (assistant village headman) and *Godet*(messenger).Equally important is the religious headman called *Naeke* and his assistant is called *Kudam Naeke*.There is a special official who is known as *Jog Manjhi*. He serves as the superintendent of the youth of the village. All these officials do not continue on a long-term basis till their death. On the day of the *Mag* festival the village officials surrender their office and the villagers evaluate the performance of their duties during the last year. If there is nothing to complain against any one of them they are asked to continue for one year more.The Santhals govern themselves and no one interferes in their governance.

This is all about one world, that is, the world consisting of villages, houses, fields, men, women, forests, etc. Beyond this world there are two other worlds, one of them is the underground world and the other is the realm of the dead up in the sky. These worlds including the world above the ground are inhabited by innumerable supernatural beings and spirits which they call *bongas*. Thus it shows that the Santhals live not only on their human tribal society but in a greater society comprising various categories of supernatural beings as well.

*Thakur Jiu* is their Supreme deity and lives in the sky. He allots a term of life to every living being and is one who is not considered a *bonga*. Next comes *Sin Chando* (sun) who is also present in the sky with the *Nindo Chando* (moon). They regulate the climatic conditions and changes in weather.

The next category of supernatural beings is the *Jaher bongas* (deities living in *jaher*-sacred grove).There are five types of *bongas* in the *jaher* which are known as national deities of the Santhals. *Maran Buru* (*bonga* of the great mountain) tops the list. Next comes *Moreko-Turuiko* (Five-Six) and *Jaher era* (lady of *jaherthan*). These three deities are installed under three *Sal* trees and they are responsible for the welfare of the village and they have control over calamities and epidemics. The other two deities are *Gosae era* and *Pargana bonga*.The former is installed under a *Mahua* tree and the latter under a Sal tree. *Gosae era* is a female deity and is a sore healer. She is worshipped by the Santhals of the *Murmu* clan as their sub-clan *bonga* and by those of *niz, gar, jugi, sada* subclans as their house *bonga*. The *Pargana bonga* has special powers over witches and is worshipped by *Ojha* and *Kudam Naeke*. Next comes *Manjhi Haram* residing at *Manjhi* than in the village. Both *Pargana* and *Manjhi bongas* have supervisory powers over other *bongas*.

These six types of deities are considered national deities.They protect the Santhals against misfortunes and calamities. When a village is polluted which happens on the occasions of birth and death these national *bongas* withdraw their protective power rendering the Santhal village vulnerable to harm and mishap caused by mischievous spirits. Pollution results not only by birth or death in the village but also by any infringement of the tribal customary laws and marriage rules. The Santhals try to remove the pollution and bring ritual purity as quickly as possible to ensure that the national deities exercise their protective power. Under special circumstances the period of death or birth pollution is reduced to get protection from the *Jaher bongas* before the malevolent spirits cause any harm to the village. Every Santhal village has its own sacred grove and the same types of national deities. But the Santhals of a particular village have no right to participate in the worship of the national *bongas* of other villages. It is the exclusive right of the Santhals of a particular village to worship the national *bongas* residing in their own *jaher*. This association of a village with the *jaher* expresses the ritual unity and social solidarity of the village.

Apart from the *Jaher bongas* or National *bongas* who take care of the Santhal as a tribe there are many other *bongas* who are associated with the Santhals at the clan and household levels. The tutelary spirits of sub-clan (*khut*) are known as *Abge bonga*. All households of a sub-clan or *khut* worship a single *Abge bonga*. Sometimes some households of a local patrilineal lineage of a sub-clan have a *Abge bonga* quite different from that of the subclan to which it belongs.Thus in some cases the *Abge bonga* is not the same for the whole *khut*. In other words, some *khuts* may have more than one *Abge bonga*. The birth of a child in a household is not the necessary condition for the child to come under the protection of the *Abge bonga* of his father's sub-clan unless the name-giving ceremony (*nim dak mandi*) is performed. The ceremony has to be observed for the child to gain formal acceptance by his father who gives the child his clan and admits him to his *bongas*. On no account a child can remain without the protection of the *bongas*. An adopted son has to undergo a ceremony called *bongatala* to adopt the *bongas* of his foster father. Unless the *bongas* of the boy are changed, he does not become his foster father's own son.

The *Abge bongas* save the members of the household from disease and distress. The names of the *Abge bongas* are kept secret.The eldest son is informed of the name of the *Abge bonga* when his father is about to die.

In order of priorities next comes the *Orak bongas* or household *bongas*. Each household or the extended families of a single patrilineage may have a single *Orak bonga*. The household *bonga* resides in the inner chamber of the house called *bhitar*. A small enclosed space is set apart inside the house for this sacred place. Married women have ritual relationship with *Orak bongas* of their husbands' households. They are not allowed to enter the *bhitar* of their parents' house. Like the *Abge bongas* the household *bongas* protect the members of the household against disease and distress.

Equally important are the *Hapramko bongas* (ancestral spirits).The ancestral spirits live in the house like the *Orak bongas* but they also have places of abode in the space between the earth and the sky. Whenever a man dies in a houshold other members say that he has become an ancestor and a *bonga*. Ancestors are believed to live with the living and , therefore, the living and the dead of the same lineage have a close relationship with one another.

So far we have seen how the *Jaher bongas* protect the Santhals as a tribe, the *Abge bongas* protect their *khut* members, the *Orak bongas* protect their household members and the *Hapramko bongas* protect their patrilineage members. It shows how neatly and orderly the *bonga* Universe is conceived. But the list of *bongas* does not end here. There is still another class of *bongas* who are as benevolent as those who are already mentioned above. The *bongas* which come under this category are called *Saket bongas* or the tutelary deities of the *ojhas* of medicinemen and diviners. The *Ojhas* are in secret communication with their tutelary *bongas* and seek their help to tackle the malevolent *bongas* who create trouble and cause illness. The *Saket bongas* have different powers. Some of them are expert in dealing with the cases of small-pox, some are concerned with madness and other types of mental derangements and still others who give relief from labour pain. When a case is referred to the *Ojha* he first detects the *bonga* causing the trouble by means of divination.Then he resorts to the processes of invoking the concerned tutelary *bonga* directing it to tackle the case. He promises to offer necessary sacrifices to the tutelary *bonga* as soon as the patient gets well.

Besides these benevolent *bongas* there are numberless malevolent *bongas* which are present in different places on earth. Some of the *bongas* of this category are *Sima bonga* (village boundary *bongas*) creating snakes, *Bahre bongas* (outskirts *bongas*) creating illusion and misguiding Santhals, *Buru bongas* (mountain *bongas*) causing damage to the crop, *Ronga Ruji bongas* (hill *bongas*), *Bagut bongas* (water *bongas*) eloping youngmen away for the sake of marrying them, *Nihar bongas* (accompanying a woman to her husband's village), *Kisar bongas* (helping a man to get rich), *bonga* husbands of witches and many stray mischievious *bongas* who are present all over the Universe. Gausdal (1960) had recorded the names of 178 different *bongas*. Bodding (1925) has recorded as many as 104 *Saket bongas* or tutelary *bongas* of *ojhas* having different powers.

The question is what is the point in giving such a lengthy description of the *bongas* and how is it relevant in the study of worldview? As it is seen bongaism occupies the core of the Santhal culture and in the Man-Nature-God three dimensional relationship greatest emphasis is laid on Gods, that is, Supernatural Beings. The *bongas* influence all aspects of Santhal life and, according to the cosmic idea of the Santhals, there is no space in the Universe which is deviod of *bongas*. The village , the house, the uplands, the fields, the underground, the sky and everywhere the *bongas* are present.

The prime concern of the *bongas* is with the Santhals. They mingle with them and interfere in their life. They appear to be with the Santhals in three different forms: (a) *bongas* with vicious behaviour, (b) *bongas* with protective behaviour, and (c) *bongas* with benevolent disposition. In such a situation the kind of attitude that the Santhals adopt towards the *bongas* is that of submission, subordination, propitiation, supplication, fear and performance or rituals which make the *bongas* feel that they are not forgotten or neglected.

The ritual observances in which the different *bongas* are offered food and drink maintain a perpetual and harmonious Man-Nature-God relationship. The *bongas* of the sacred grove and the boundary and field *bongas* are offered food and drink and worshipped on the occasion of the *Erok* festival when paddy seeds are sown broadcast. These *bongas* are also worshipped on the occasion of the *Hariar* festival so that they make the paddy plants grow green. Before eating the first millet crop and first paddy crop and fruits which ripen at this time, a festival called *Irigundli* is observed in the month of September to propitiate the National *bongas*. *Sohrae* festival is observed during December - January to express thankfulness and gratitude to the *bongas* for the bumper harvest. Before cutting thatching grass in the month of March the *Mag* festivel is celebrated to worship all the *bongas* and pray to them for protection against calamities. The *Mahua* flowers are not eaten and Sal flowers are not worn unless *Baha parab* is celebrated in the month of March to offer sacrifice to the *Jaher bongas*. There are many such rituals and festivals observed by the Santhals one after another to show respect and reverence to the *bongas* and assure them that they are not neglected. This is how a harmonious relationship between Man-Nature-God is maintained and blessings and good wishes of the *bongas* obtained for leading a happy and healthy life.

## REFERENCES

Archer, W.G., 1974, *The Hill of Flutes : Life, Love and Poetry in Tribal India ( A Portrait of the Santals )*, London:George Allen & Unwin.

Bodding, Paul Olaf, 1925, "The Santals and Disease", *Memoirs of the Asiatic Society of Bengal,* Calcutta.10 (1), pp.1-132

Culshaw, W.J., 1939, "Some Notes on Bongaism", *Journal of the Asiatic Society of Bengal (Letters),* Calcutta, 5, pp.427-31.

Datta-Majumdar, Nabendu, 1956, *The Santal: A Study in Culture-Change,* Calcutta Govt. Of India Press.

Elwin, Verrier, 1955, *Religion of an Indian Tribe,* Bombay: Oxford University Press.

Evans-Pritchard, E.E., (ed). 1954, *The Institutions of Primitive Society,* Oxford : Basil Blackwell.

____________, 1956, *Nuer Religion,* Oxford : Clarendon Press.

____________, 1965, *Theories of Primitive Religion,* Oxford : Clarendon Press.

Gausdal, Johannes, 1960, *The Santal Khuts,* Osol : H. Aschchoug & Co.

Majumdar, Dhirendra Nath, 1937, *A Tribe in Transition : A Study in Culture Pattern,* London : Longmans Green & Co.

Malinowski, Bronislaw, 1954, *Magic, Science and Religion and other Essays,* New York : Doubleday Anchor Books.

____________, 1965, *Coral Gardens and their Magic,* 2 Vols., Bloomington: Indiana University Press.

Man, E.G., 1867, *Sonthalia and the Sonthals,* Calcutta : Geo Wyman & Co.

Mukherjea, Charulal, 1962, *The Santhals,* Calcutta : A Mukherjee & Co. Pvt. Ltd., 2nd revised edition.

O'Malley, L.S.S., 1910, *Bengal District Gazetteers,* Vol.22, Santal Parganas, Calcutta: Bengal Secretariat Book Depot.

Redfield, R., 1962, *The Human Nature and the Study of Society,* The University of Chicago Press.

# 15

# SANTHAL WORLDVIEW WOVEN AROUND RICE AND BANANA CULTIVATION

*S. K. Chakraborty*

---

The Santhals of West Bengal and Bihar are a settled agricultural community. In addition to agriculture, occasional hunting and gathering in the adjoining forest, labour work, domestication, fishing, small business, tailoring etc., are some of their occupations. The Santhals are a patrilocal people. They are divided into a number of clans such as *Hembram, Murmu, Baske, Soren, Tudu, Marndi* and others. Each division within the community is referred to by the term *paris* by them.

Rice is the major cultivated crop of the Santhals in the eastern part of India. Banana — one of the fruit producing plants is also cultivated by a number of Santhals in the recent days. In connection with the agricultural activities they have various ideas, beliefs and attitudes about the Universe they live in. In this paper an attempt has been made to highlight some of these ideas.

## Land and the Soil

Rice is the staple food and major crop of the Santhal in the eastern part of India. In a study of three villages of West Bengal and Bihar named Goghat, Phulboni and Kanchanbera, it was found that majority of them cultivate rice. Those who were not cultivators expressed their desire to grow rice if land, economic resources for purchasing seeds and fertilizers were available to them.

The Santhals of West Bengal and Bihar use the term *bodh* or *khet* to refer to their agricultural land. The Santhals of Midnapore (now Medinipur) district of West Bengal divide their agricultural land into three categories : (i) *usul* or *ghutu bodh* (dry highland), (ii) *gahir* or *latar bodh* (deep low lying land) and (iii) *sole bodh* (middle land). Similarly, the Santhals of Dumka district of Bihar classify their land into four types : (i) *sathi khet* (very high land at the connecting homestead), (ii) *bodh khet* (dry high land below the homestead area), (iii) *baihar* or *bohal khet* (deep low lying land) and (iv) *canali khet* (middle land between high dry land and deep low lying land).

The Santhals in West Bengal refer to the soil of their agricultural land and the soil around their settlements by the term *hansa. Hansa* is of four types : (i) *antiar hansa* (clay), (ii) *bali hansa* (sand), (iii) *donash hansa* (loam) and *poly hansa* (silt)

The Santhals of Dumka district of Bihar classify the agricultural soil into five categories. These are : (i) *gobrao hansa* (fine sandy soil around the territorial boundary of homestead area), (ii) *goda hansa* (coarse sandy soil mixed with fine granules outside the homestead fence), (iii) *bodh hansa* (coarse sand mixed with red soil and some amount of white, red and black pebbles just below the *goda hansa*), (iv) *canali hansa* (black coloured soil mixed with sand and white, red and black pebbles below *bodh hansa ),* (v) *bohal hansa* (black coloured soil mixed with little sand and little white, red and black coloured pebbles).

In the *gobrao hansa,* paddy does not grow sufficiently as the coarse sandy soil is mixed with white granules and scanty red soil. In this soil, rice of a wild grass — like variety, viz. *janhay* is cultivated. In the *bodh hansa,* local varieties of rice, viz. *bodh huru* and *ashnia sathi* are cultivated. In the *canali hansa* crops grow better than in the *bodh hansa* which is situated just below it and has the capacity of holding rainwater for a long time. In this soil the Santhals cultivate rice which they know as *lal sarna.* In the *bohal hansa* rice cultivation is facilitated as the nature of the soil and land type are conducive to it. The varieties of rice cultivated in this soil are: *dhusuri huru, radha, aul huru, padma huru,* etc.

Rice is called *huru* by the Santhals. The different varieties of rice cultivated by them are divided into three major categories. These are : (a) *aus,* (b) *aman* and (c) *boro.* The different varieties of *aus* category are known as *kari aus, tusko aus, masori, amrapaloi, bhutmuria aus, eri, pusa* etc.; those of *aman* are: *sunya kalma, suya dahar, lekraisal, sadaisal, hazarnai, hazar dash, nuna, kaya, jata, vimsal, sitasal,* etc.; and of *boro* are *I.R. Chhatrish, baisotetrish, parijat, anna purna, china boro* etc.

## Rice Cultivation and Consumption Pattern

Soil preparation, sowing or transplantation, irrigation, manuring, weeding, application of insecticides, harvesting, guarding, threshing, winnowing and storing are the general processes followed by the Santhals in cultivation of rice.

Ploughing is done three to four times according to the nature of the land. Sowing or transplantation of the *aus* variety is done in the month of *Vaisakha* (April-May) or sometimes *Jyaistha* (May-June) and the harvesting operation is completed in the month of *Sravana* (July-August), *Bhadrapada* (August-September) and sometimes *Asvina* (September-October). Sowing or transplantation of the *aman* variety is done in the months of *Jyaistha* (May-June), *Asadha* (June-July) or sometimes *Sravana* (July-August) and harvesting is completed in the month of *Agrahayana* (November-December) or *Pausa* (December-January). Transplantation of *boro* paddy is completed in the month of *Magha* (January-February) and harvesting is done in the month of *Vaisakha* (April-May).

Husked rice is of two types. The boiled type is known as *takay chaulay* and the unboiled type is *adoa chaulay.* The first one is used in day-to-day life as an essential food material cooked in various ways. The second one is used in rituals both at individual and community levels. The Santhals of West Bengal and Bihar say *setabela* or *baskia bela* to mark the time beginning from sunrise to about 8 A.M. This is the time when they cook rice and eat it fresh with starch. This food is known as *baskia,* i.e. morning meal. The time from 8 A.M. to 1 P.M. is known as *tikin*. This time they consume the excess rice cooked in the morning. It is known as *majan,* i.e. midday meal. The time from 1 P.M. to that before the setting of the sun is known *as aiub bir.* The time changes from noon to afternoon is called *tara sing.* This time they usually do not take any food. The time after sunset, i.e. from 7 P.M. to 9 P.M., is known as *aiub.* During this time, the Santhals cook rice again. They also extract the starch from the cooked rice and consume it. It is known as *kendo,* i.e. night meal. The time from 10 P.M. to 2 P.M. is known as *ehum ningday.* This is the sleeping time of the Santhals. They hear the cry of their domestic fowl at 3 A.M. This time is called *simra* when they are awake and rise from the bed. Then they wash their hands and feet. The early morning hour, from 5 A.M. to 6 A.M., is known as *seta.* At this time they start their day's work.

Rice starch (*da-ter*), fried rice (*khajori*), flattened rice (*taben*) are also occasionally consumed by the Santhals. Ricebeer (*handi*) is a very common drink. It also finds place in the rituals of Santhals in eastern India. Powdered form of husked rice (*holong*) is used to prepare different types of cake. This cake is offered to their deities and also consumed by them.

## Banana Cultivation

The Santhals use the term *kaira darey* to refer to the banana plants while the fruit is known as *kaira.* Banana plantation in large areas is not found among the Santhals in the eastern part of India. They do, however, grow this tree in area around their houses. Bananas cultivated by the Santhals are of three types : (i) *Patiay kaira kanchkala* — a green plantation (ii) *bili* or *chini kaira* (a small variety of banana offered to the deities) and (iii) *jang kaira* (*bichaykala* — a variety of banana used as a vegetable).

The Santhals choose the soft soil enriched with organic matter or mud depostis on a small plot of land adjoining their huts for banana plantation. The spot is sometimes situated near a well (*kuyo*), pond, etc., where the soil is naturally more fertile. Banana plantation is done during the monsoon season mainly in the month of *Asadha* (June-July) or *Sravana* (July-August). They collect the saplings from the neighbours, kin members or anywhere from the locality. The cultivation of bananas primarily consists of digging pits, applying mud and ash of cow dung in it, planting of banana sapling or seed, applying oil-cake, salt or sometimes chemical fertilizers for growth, removal of suckers and replantation, cutting of dry leaves and support for the fruit-bearing plants, applying B.H.C. powder, Democrin, etc. at the growing stage, and harvesting mother plant at the matured fruit-bearing stage.

Both unripe and ripe bananas are important sources of food to the Santhals. *Patiay kaira* (*kanch kala*) is a nutritious diet of the Santhals. It is particularly helpful in alleviating fever and some other ailments by those suffering from fever. *Jang kaira* is also consumed as a vegetable while the *chini kaira* is offered to their deities occasionally. The spathe of plantain (*kaira maja*) and plantain flower (*kaira baha*) are consumed by the Santhals as cooked vegetables.

**Worldview**

Earth : The Santhals refer to the earth as *ath*. Before its formation the earth was submerged in water. The supreme God and Goddess, viz.*Thakur* and *Thakrani*, created one gander and one goose from the grime of their body. These two birds were flying in the sky for 12 years as there was no land. So, the *Thakur* created the earth with the help of an earthworm (*kenchua Raj*). Those two birds sat on this earth. They laid two eggs and from these two human creatures originated. One is known as *Pilcu Haram* (male) and the other is known as *Pilcu Budhi* (female). They are believed to be the progenitors of the Santhals. This human couple gave birth to seven males and seven females. They married each other and thus different ethnic groups were originated from their stock. The earth is considered to be a Mother Goddess, viz. *Basuki bashkmata* or *Dharti* by the Santhals. They build their huts on the earth. Rituals and festivals are held on the earth. Agricultural products, good or bad, depend on the nature of the earth. *Maran Buru*, the elder son of the Supreme God, levelled the earth with a ladder known as *argom.* He pushed the soil from east to west and then to north. Thus at the region where much soil deposited hill was formed and where deposition was scanty plain was formed.

The Santhals perceived that during the formation of hill and plain, plains were to be convered into agricultural land for producing cereals for the satisfaction of their hunger. In Santhal opinion, agricultural land is the most valuable resource as it is everlasting and does not change like the material items. It gives wealth as much as the owner or worker can devote time and labour to it.

Water Sources : The Santhals refer to water as *da*. It is of various types, viz. (i) water of rain — *sermada,* (ii) water of river — *naida*, (iii) water of canal — *garada,* (iv) water of pond — *pukrida,* (v) water of ringwell — *kuida,* (vi) water of tubewell — *kalda* and (vii) water of sea — *dariada.*

a. *Canal* : Most of the Santhals believe that the canal is an important source of irrigation of their agricultural land. Their concept is that rain water flows from the upward to the downward direction continuously and digs up the earth and forms the canals.

b. *River :* The Santhals believe that the water of many sources, viz. rainwater, water of canal and that from agricultural field flows continuously and forms a big river. River is known as *nai* and considered to be an important source of water to the Santhals.

c. *Pond :* Regarding the formation of ponds the Santhals believe that once upon a time there was some depressed land in and around their settlements. They felt a necessity for bath and, drinking water for their domesticated cattles. So they sat together and decided to build a pond. Pond is known as *pukri*.

d. *Ringwell :* Ringwell is an important source of water in most of the Santhal villages. They believe that to fulfil human needs the Supreme God brought an iron bar and an elephant known as *gajamatihati* from heaven to this earth with the help of a spider who supplied a long cord. Coming down on this earth the elephant of the heaven put pressure on the iron bar with his foot. The iron bar pierced the earth till it touched hell. In this way a ringwell was set up.

e. *Rain :* The Santhals use the term *rimil* for the clouds in the sky. They say that the rain water known as *sermada* comes down to the earth from *rimil*. *Rimils* are of three kinds: (i) *pnur rimil,* i.e. white-coloured cloud, (ii) *ara rimil,* i.e. red-coloured cloud, and (iii) *hnaday rimil,* i.e. black-coloured cloud. They believe that *pnur rimil* and *hnaday rimil* cause rainfall and there is maximum rainfall when these two *rimils* get mixed up. Their experience is that medium rainfall is good for their agriculture, and long spells of heavy rainfall cause flood which is known as *ban.* It destorys their crops.

f. *Hail :* Some Santhals believe that the vapour of water arrives on the *rimil* and is converted into ice. When the ice melts it drops on the earth as rain (*sermada*). But when it does not melt it falls on the earth as hail. Few Santhals believe that in the heaven, Rama Chandra, the hero of the *Ramayana,* shoots arrows at Ravana, the king of Lanka. A flash of lightning indicates the spot where Ravana stands. Clouds of both the sides strike each other and produce fire some of which comes down on the earth as a thunder bolt. A bit of fire comes down to the earth as hail. The dust particles of the heaven come down to the earth as rain.

g. *Mist and Dew :* A number of Santhals believe that vapour comes out of the water in the earth and goes to the sky. It is deposited there and after a certain period of time it drops on the earth as mist and dew. It is mostly seen in the winter season. Mist is locally known as *kuhora* and dew as *sisirda.* Heavy mist is harmful for the crops while the dew is helpful for the healthy growth of ears of the corn.

Fire : The Santhals believe that fire originated from the heat produced by the rubbing of two pieces of wood. At present they produce fire with the matches. During agricultural operations they keep fire for smoking in the paddy field.

Forest : The forest is known as *bir.* The Santhals believe that when *Thakur*, the Supreme God, created the earth, plants were also created by him. The Santhals built their huts in some places on the earth while some other parts were lying vacant for various types of plants to grow. The plants gradually grew and thus a forest was produced. The forest is an important resource to them as they obtain many things ranging from firewood to food materials from it.

Rice : A number of Santhals believe that at an early stage all the rice grains were in an unhusked form, without any sheath known as *chaulay*. One day a beggar came to a Santhal household. A member of that household gave him some unhusked rice. When returning from that household the beggar again took some unhusked rice from the paddy field on his own. The Supreme God became unhappy at this and covered the *chaulay* with a sheath. Since then, the rice grains are hidden in sheaths.

## Man-Nature Relationship

The Santhals have very close ties with nature which exists around the human society. It consists of various small and large natural bodies which are described below. The Santhals believe that at first the position of the sky was very near to the head. A woman belonging to the caste of Hari was facing obstacles in touching the sky with her head. So, she became annoyed with it and struck, the sky with the broomstick. Thus the sky was raised above in long stretches. It is known as *rimil.* It gives rain to the earth and thus accelerates the growth of their agriculture.

The Santhals' conception about the sun and the moon is that they are husband and wife. The sun is known as *Sin Chando* while the moon is called *Nindo Chandò. Sin Chando* functions during daytime and gives them sunlight (*situm*) which helps them to move about, get to their place of work. It also indicates the time when they should stop work. In the same way *Nindo Chando* gives light at night. As a result, the Santhals can find their way at that time too. They believe that both the sun and the moon originated at the same place where the cloud (*rimil*) originated.

The moon's full form observed in the sky at night is known as *kunami.* From this time the period of a fortnight is known as *ter-dei-nido.* The Santhals consider this time as a period of happiness because they can easily do all kinds of work at this time and fulfill all their desires and wants. On the contrary, due to the disappearance of the moon from the sky darkness appears and from this time a period of a fortnight is known as *nutotnido.* This time is considered to be a period of sorrow as they cannot do their work easily for want of light and thus suffer from domestic wants. A number of Santhals believe that when the days of the new moon are over, the moon, in a small size, is observed in the west corner of the sky. They count this time as the beginning of a new month. They utter the name of *Sin Chando* and *Nindo Chando* when they are falsely implicated.

During the time of the solar and lunar eclipse the Santhals think that once upon a time the sun or the moon incurred a debt from *Dom Raja*, a king of the heaven, and they could not repay the debt. So, *Dom Raja* (king) caught hold of them which is the cause of the solar and lunar eclipse. They utter *horibol* at this time in the same manner as at the time of cremation. They believe that if bows, arrows, sticks and spears are preapared at this time, they become functionally good for the future.

To the Santhals, the star is known as *epil.* They say that different types of stars are seen in the sky. An evening star is known as *nazam epil.* A large star is distinctly confined at night and it is known as *nido epil.* Similarly, another large star arises on the sky at dawn. It is known as *bhurka epil.* They determine the changes in the night by looking at the position of these stars. From the appearance of *bhurka epil,* i.e. the star of dawn, for example, the Santhals decide that they need not keep awake any more for guarding their agricultural crops. There was least possibility of a thief coming to their fields.

The Santhals sometimes see the constellation of seven stars in the sky at night. This is the great bear. They believe that a mother of seven Santhal brothers is dead. So, four brothers out of the seven carry their mother on a cot and the remaining three carry an earthen pot, a lighted, twisted straw rope and a spade in their hands. They keep walking over the sky continuously and yet cannot reach the spot where their mother would be cremated.

Sometimes at night the milky way is stretched over the sky. The Santhals in their own villages use a path along which they go to the grazing ground or agricultural field with their domestic buffalos and cattles. This path is known to them as *kanra-dahar-ai dahar*. A number of Santhals, observing the milky way in the sky, think that a similar path has been stretched over the earth.

The Santhals of West Bengal and Bihar believe that there are some supernatural beings who control their destiny. In the causes of sufferings, misfortunes, and mishaps, these supernatural beings have a hand. They believe that these supernatural beings are both benevolent and malevolent in nature. They give them courage, strength, wealth, peace and harmony on both individual and community levels. Similarly, troubles and sufferings may come, if the supernatural beings are displeased with them. Some of the benevolent deities of the Santhals are *Maran Buru*, *Jaher era, Moreko-Turuiko, Sima bonga*, etc. The Santhals propitiate them for good agricultural products or trouble-free harvesting. Both at individual family level and community level they are worshipped by the Santhals at different times of the year. A number of deities, viz. *Karam*, *Bagut*, etc., are considered malevolent in nature and thus they are propitiated by them purely out of fear.

The Santhals have a strong belief in their ancestral spirits that are considered to be well-wishers of the Santhal family and so protect them from any harmful effect. Ancestral spirits are known as *haram buro* and *haram buri*. During *Sohrae* and *Maram parab* festivals and any other occasions of domestic rituals, the ancestral spirits are worshipped with profound respect.

The concept of ghosts and evil spirits is another characteristic feature of the Santhals. They are propitiated by the Santhals out of fear. Such type of ghosts or evil spirits are known as *Dahini, Joka, Bagut,* etc.

The Santhals are fully conscious of their in-group solidarity. This solidarity is observed when they specifically point out Munda, Kora, Lodha, Mahali, Mahara and Diku to the people in their locality other than the Santhals. They feel proud to introduce themselves by the term *adibasi* or *Santhal* who belong to *Adim kheros-al* i.e. the first residents of the country. Every Santhal individual is supposed to participate in the community festivals like *Sohrae*, *Maram parab*, etc. Similarly, in the case of a danger, mishap or misfortune of a person, it affects the whole group. Thus a close tie is observed in man-to-man relationship within the community where each and every person is attached with each other by sentimental ties.

To sum up, it is clear that the Santhals are a self-styled ethnic group in the eastern part of India. Hence, geography, occupation and culture have some correlation which is observed in their way of life. Many of their ideas, beliefs, tales or thought processes are correlated with the social structure of this community.

## REFERENCES

Adhikary, A.K., 1984, *Society and World View of the Birhor : A Nomadic Hunting and Gathering Community of Orissa,* Calcutta : Anthropological Survey of India, Govt. of India.

Horton, Robin, 1962, The Kalahari World View : An outline and their interpretation, *Africa*, Vol.32, pp. 197-220.

Jones, W. T., 1972, World View: Their nature and their function, *Current Anthropology,* Vol.13, No.I, pp. 79-109.

Lewis, Oscar, 1958, *Village Life in Northern India: Studies in a Delhi Village,* Urbana : University of Illinois Press.

Mandelbaum, David, G.,1961, 'The World and the World View of the Kota', in Mckim Morriott (Ed.), *Village India* (First Indian Printing), Bombay: Asia Publishing House, pp. 228-260.

Mehra, J. D.,1977, 'The World View of Indian Tribes', in S. C. Dube (Ed.) *Tribal*

*Heritage of India,* Vol.I, pp.58-84, New Delhi : Vikas Publishing House Pvt.Ltd.

Morab, S. G., 1982, 'Values and World View of the Nomadic Kille-Kyatha' in P.K. Misra and K.C.Malhotra (Ed.) *Nomads in India,* Calcutta : Anthropological Survey of India, Govt. of India.

Sills, David L., 1968, World View. *International Encyclopaedia of the Social Sciences* (Ed.), Vol.16, The Macmillan Company and the Free Press. pp.576-579.

# 16

# CHANGE AND CONTINUITY IN SANTHAL WORLDVIEW

*Sachchidananda*

In social reality dichotomies in terms of continuity and change have no more than a heuristic value. Indian experience after Independence has clearly demonstrated that there is a lack of fit between modernization objectives and their acceptance by the masses, resulting in confusion (Dube, 1988:23)[1]. Some modernist thinkers regard development in culture's own premises a contradiction in terms and lament its passing away as the price of progress (Badley, 1982)[2]. They tend to overlook that in the limited social space people are both the definers and the defined (Archer, 1987:13)[3]. Social thinkers and planners forgot that change is a composite process of acceptance and rejection.

In view of the fast changes taking place in the enviornment of the tribal world , the worldview of the tribals assumes salience. Sol Tax on the basis of his study in Guatemala defines it as the mental apprehension of reality which includes the entire corpus of knowledge and beliefs about nature and man (Sol Tax, 1994: 27, 42).[4] According to Redfield the worldview of a people is the way people characteristically look outward upon the Universe. Worldview suggests how everything looks to a people, the designation of the existence as a whole. It includes conception of what ought to be as well as what is, patterns of thought and the affective and cognitive aspects of these things. It cannot be conceived without some dimension of time, some idea of the past and the future, their emotional life, contemplation or required disposition and their capacity to identify themselves with the rest of the cosmos (Redfield, 1955).[5] Geertz views this concept as a people's picture of the way things in their sheer actuality are, their concept of nature of self and of society. It contains their most comprehensive ideas of order (Geertz, 1968 :307).[6]

The common denominator of all these definitions involves the beliefs and behaviour of a community, its cosmology, environment — some verbalized, some not, with reference to a time dimension and some relationship of all these with social forms which determine the place of man in nature and society in terms more implicit than explicit.

## II

The Santhal cosmos comprises divinities, spirits called *bongas* and human beings. They are in constant interaction with each other. The creator of the Universe, *Thakur Jiu* allots each Santhal a term of life but rarely interferes in day-to-day affairs. *Sin Chando* organizes days and nights and is responsible for heat and cold and rain and sunshine. He promotes health and happiness. Underneath the sun and beneath the clouds, the Santhal is challenged by *bongas*. Only by coming to terms with them can a Santhal be happy.

The *bongas* are believed to reside in three domains: (i) the upland, forest, etc., (ii) the 'realm of the dead' located in the sky and above the village. Each person after the conclusion of his death rites enters this domain, (iii) *bongas* living in the village on trees, hills , rocks, and air as well as individual houses. Such spirits include the *Sima bonga,* the *Bir bonga,* the *Buru bonga,* the *Dari bonga.* Besides these the other *bongas* are the *Bhitar bonga, Abge bonga, Pargana bonga* and the *bonga* associated with *Manjhi Haram* (the founder head of the village).

Then there are *bongas* who are not confined to one place. They are nameless. They cause sickness. Such *bongas* are

NACHOR *bongas,* Hindu festival *bonga,* and the *Kisar bonga* who help people to get rich. All these *bongas* are the creation of the Santhal mind and are concerned only with the Santhal. They are completely unconcerned about other communities living in the Santhal village. They are vitally involved in everything a Santhal does. Some of these *bongas* constantly interfere with their lives. These are of three kinds :

(i) Those who are capable of sudden vicious behaviour such as the *Sima bonga,* the Hindu festival *bonga,* the *Orak bonga.* The *bonga* associated with the hills, forest and streams create a sudden feeling of insecurity.

(ii) Those who are largely protective and well disposed such as the *Abge bonga,* the *Maran Buru bonga* and the spirits associated with the *jaher* or the sacred grove.

(iii) Those who are desperately concerned with tribal welfare and integrity. These include the Great or the National *bonga.* If such bongas are outraged the very foundation of Santhal life crumbles. "To pass their days happily and to experience the full joy of tribal existence, the Santhal must not only attune themselves to village customs but unite in honouring their ghostly protectors" (Archer, 1974 : 29) . It is indeed a double world which the Santhal encounters, a world at once visible as also invisible. The *bongas* have to be propitiated at the individual and also at the village level.At the time of meals or in religious rites, some food has to be set apart for these invisible beings. Due prominence, however, is given to such propitiation at the village level, particularly at the time of the various festivals which mark the agricultural calendar.

The invocation to the *bonga* at the *Erok* festival celebrated every year in July after seeds for sowing are broadcast reflects the expectations of the Santhal from these invisible spirits.

"Take this in the name of the Erok festival.
Where we sow may twelve shoots come,
Let there be rain and storm,
May the fields be flooded,

Let no illness, no ache of belly or head enter the village,
Bear all sickness away,
If there are widows or women of bad omen, frown on them, show
them no favour,
Keep us from all harm,
May the cattle roam at will,
Protect them with your covering hood."[8]

Similar invocations are made at different festivals such as *Sohrae*, *Mag* and *Baha*. It is believed that all the festivals are performed with the customary rituals associated with them. The worst expression of *bonga* malice can be averted and they can be induced to maintain their protective care. Care should also be taken that the *bonga* is not polluted. After each birth or death, there is a period of pollution for the household. Pollution may also be caused by transgression of the tribal rule prohibiting incest within the clan or any sexual relationship between a Santhal and a person hailing from some other community. It is, therefore, most important that purification ceremony is performed to wipe off the pollution. The *bonga* constitutes not a mere alien hierarchy, and when hostile, they act like demons. This is the Santhal reaction to the mystery of existence, its sudden calamities, abrupt hazards and chances. When benign, they represent all that the tribal actually values. The National *bongas* are the guardians of faith, the arm of an unalterable law. They assist Santhals to be themselves and by the active interaction sustain welfare and morale[9] (Archer, 1974 : 31).

In the Santhal psyche annual hunt is extremely important. It may be only a ritual due to the disappearance of the forest in their neighbourhood. It is at this time that unsettled disputes between villages are discussed by the tribal elders. The evenings are regaled with songs and dances. It is indeed the most important event of the year. It signifies the loyalty of the Santhal to their tribe, promotes their cohesion as well as the distinctive identity. Within the village the Santhal is self-governing with the institutions of the headman and the tribal panchayat. They see to it that within the village the Santhal govern the Santhal.

The various rites and rituals performed by the Santhal ensure the safety and prosperity of the community. They also give an opportunity to the people for rejoicing and merry-making. The rituals are symbolic expressions of the collective sentiments of a society. This is evident from certain common symbols whose presence in all ceremonies is quite noticeable. The libations and sacrificial offerings which are shared by the people and the spirits are an expression of the presence and fellowship with spirits. The villagers get together for the worship of the *bongas* and each household contributes a share of the sacrificial offerings. The collective sacrificial eating and drinking with these spirits, and sacred places where these rituals are performed at the time of festivals indicate the special presence of the spirits and of their intervention.

The rituals also symbolize emphatically the dependence of the Santhal on *bongas*. The oblation in the sacrificial offerings and the invocations made by *Naeke* on behalf of the whole village symbolized the acknowledgement of the control of the *bongas* over their life. When a new crop is harvested, the first fruits are offered to the *bonga.* Everyone can use the grain only after this. The rejoicing and festivity in most festivals can take place only after the *bongas* are propitiated. In case *bongas* have been defiled by either birth or death in a village, no festivity can take place unless the pollution is removed.

Another symbolic element that is noticeable is the sense of new life and harmony and nature. The indifferent seasons of the year demonstrate this amply. The *Baha* signifies new life when nature is blooming. Similarly *Sohrae* and *Janthar* festivals symbolize new life and abundance. The throb of new life is also manifested in the purificatory bath which is taken by all villagers before every rite and festival. The new life also extends to the surroundings. The house is white-washed, courtyard and the cattle shed are cleaned, the village street and the sacred places are also given a new look. The harmony with nature is manifested in the fact that most of the village festivals are connected with the cycle of seasons and the agricultural calendar.

The idea of community solidarity is expressed in collective feasting, drinking, singing, dancing, mutual visits and exchange of gifts. All these festivals are occasions of unbounded joy. The Santhal's experience and expression of joy is evident not only from his existence as an individual but also as a member of the community. The festivals stimulate the collective sentiment of the Santhal. Everyone becomes conscious about the unity of the social group and his dependence on the spirits. They are indeed techniques for entering into communion with the invisible world.[10] The collective celebrations are to perpetuate the values that the community holds dear. They underline their identity as Santhal. At a recent conference of the Santhal, a delegate expressed his feelings in the following words :

> "We have suffered a lot due to the changing time but such festivals are sacrosanct. They are rooted in our tradition and we must cling to them"[11] (*The Statesman,* Calcutta, April 28, 1978 : 7).

### III

Santhals organize their activities in consonance with the natural environment and the changing seasons. They have their own names for the different seasons. There are also terms for day and night as also for the different days of the week. They have adopted the names from the Hindu calendar for the different months.

Santhals do not have an abstract concept of time. They reckon time mostly in concrete terms, the knowledge[12] of which is shared by all people. Evans-Pritchard has conceived of two kinds of time among the Nuer. The first, 'ecological time' is defined as reflection of their relations to environment. The second, 'structural time' represents reflection of their relations to one another in the social structure. In Evans-Pritchard's terminology the Santhal recognize 'ecological time.'

Like other tribesmen, a Santhal is rarely bothered about time. He cannot become a slave to the time machine. He does not value it as money or a source of wealth. His own idea of a good life does not give it much importance. A whole village may spend the entire day running after a wounded pigeon hopping from tree to tree with the fond hope to catch it when it falls (Mahapatra,1992:129)[13]. They may also spend the whole day in going to and coming back from the weekly market without having anything to buy or sell.

## IV

A large number of Santhals live in mixed villages constituted of a number of other communities, some belonging to the scheduled tribes, some to the scheduled castes and others to Hindu castes, both high and low. The Santhals, however, constitute the dominant population of these villages. With these social groups they are in constant interaction in the ordinary business of life. They are dependent on some of these groups for essential services, without which is not possible for them to carry on their social and economic activities.

Among such communities, there are Santhals who have been converted to Christianity. They are completely alienated from the dominant village population. Their entire life, attitudes and beliefs are different from those of their unconverted brethren. They do not participate in the Santhal communal rituals and festivals.This estranged group has eroded social cohesion in the village.

In some areas, the Santhal live with the Paharia. Two of the branches of this tribe, viz. Sauria Paharia and Mal Paharia, figure in the Scheduled Tribe list. The most advanced section of this community are the Kumarbhag Paharia who have been listed as a backward community.The Sauria Paharia are traditionally shifting cultivators on the hills or the hill-top villages. Only some of them have taken to settled cultivation on the plains land. The Mal Paharia have taken to settled cultivation, although their agricultural practices are 'backward' as compared to those of the Santhal. There is no love lost between the Santhal and the Sauria Paharia. They have been castigated as looters or marauders by the Santhal.Now the Sauria Paharia have retreated to the hills and are afraid of the Santhal.

The Mahali and the Turi are traditionally basket makers. The dialects they speak are akin to Santhali. They also work as daily wage labourers. They maintain some social distance from the Turi and consider them untouchable. Among the scheduled caste groups in a Santhal village mention may be made of the Bhiya who claim to be Rajputs. The Dom and the Mochi figure at the bottom of the social hierarchy. The Kamar or Lohar work as blacksmiths and carpenters. Santhals are dependent on them for making their iron and wooden implements.The potter's work is done by the Pal community. Pasi are the toddy-tappers while the Tanti work as cloth weavers.

A community which stands between Hindu and Muslim is the *Jadupatua*. They are the magic painters. During mediumistic seances they draw pictures of the Santhals who had died recently and act as intermediaries between the Santhal and the other world (Dutt, 1957:32).[14]

Besides these groups, on some villages of the Santhal we find high caste Hindus. There are two kinds of Brahmins, the local or the Rarhi Brahmins and the Maithil Brahmins who have migrated from North Bihar. At some places the Kanyakubj Brahmins are also found. Some groups claim to be Kshatriyas as they have, at some point of time, been rulers. In some villages we also find Kayasthas, who traditionally worked as village accountants and as petty government officers and professionals. The community with which the Santhal had the closest interaction is the Bhagats who are shopkeepers, traders, grain merchants as well as moneylenders.

In the Santhal psyche these different groups fall into two main categories. Some are regarded as friendly and the others as hostile (Gautam, 1977 : 37)[15]. The friendly groups are those functional groups in the Santhal village who act as a support to the Santhal social organization and economy and without whom the Santhal cannot lead a happy life. These groups speak Santhali and interact with them on equal terms.They share their joys and sorrows and take an active part in their festivals.Unlike these groups are higher caste Hindu groups who are originally plains dwellers and migrants to the Santhal area. They are considered to be outsiders. The Santhal have not forgotten their chicanery and exploitation. Hence the Santhal's relations with them are hostile and tense. They are avoided on social occasions. These outsiders are addressed as the *Diku*. They are, in fact, hated by the Santhal and both the communities remain in a state of unceasing confrontation.

It has been observed earlier that the worldview of a people is not timeless. Its different components, however, react to forces of change differently. The interrelation of various aspects of the Santhal culture does not mean that they are not autonomous in some respects. The introduction of windows in the Santhal house, of tomato cultivation, changes in the manner of greeting and the adoption of the Hindu Goddess Kali in their pantheon has not given rise to a corresponding change in their worldview. On the other hand the spread of education in Santhal society combined with the increasing acquaintance with modern industries is reflected in the Santhal worldview (Dutta Majumdar, 1955 : 124)[16].

Another change in the worldview seems to be the greater importance being attached to time, the sequence as well as the duration. It has been pointed out that the prime mover for the change over to industrial ethic was a timepiece rather than the steam engine[17]. It has been observed that wherever the Santhal are employed as daily wage workers either in the agricultural sector or in the industrial setting, *ponga* and *pagar* (siren and daily wage) have become very important for them. Unless they reach their place of employment on time, they cannot claim full wages. It has sometimes been seen that the modernization of agriculture which demands timely intercultural operations came into conflict with the ritualistic basis of agriculture. In most places, however, this has been amicably resolved.

Increasing contacts with Hindu population over a long period of time have led to the introduction of a large number of Hindu gods and goddesses in the Santhal pantheon. Each Hindu festival has been associated with a *bonga* and all these gods are clubbed together in the category of Hindu festival *bonga.* There is another class of *bongas* known as *Deki bonga* or the gods associated with the *Diku*. Although the relationship between the Santhal and the *Diku* has always been hostile, a number of Hindu gods and goddesses are propitiated by the Santhal. These are Kali, Durga, Ganga Mai, Laxmi, Mahadeo, Parvati, Rama and Krishna. The *Chhat* festival is observed in many parts of the Santhal land with the worship of the *Chhat bonga.* In fact, the leader of the Kherwar movement, Bhagirath, identified Ram with *Chando*. He also closely followed Hindu ideas of purity and pollution , Bhagirath's teachings were popularized by Dubiya Gosain in the early eighties of the last century. In 1897 the Sapha Hor group split from the Kherwar movement. This group was inspired by the concept of purity and pollution. Its followers wore the sacred thread, gave up liquor or eating of meat and took a purificatory bath before the first meal. It has been pointed out that the institution of the *Ojha* or the spirit healer in Santhal villages has been imported from Hindu villages. The Santhal have no objection to the inclusion of new gods and goddesses in his pantheon and some festivals in his annual calendar as these do not require giving up the traditional beliefs and practices. May be they also believed that these new *bongas* would help tide over the crises caused by the failure of their own gods and spirits to protect them from exploitation and economic ruin.

With the passage of time , the migration of opportunist merchants, timber traders, liquor sellers, moneylenders and land-hungry immigrants in the land of the Santhal, the process of their expropriation from land and forest was accelerated. The Santhal were famed for reclaiming land from the forest and making it fit for agriculture. In course of time with their chronically deficit economy and unbridled social expenses and drinking habits, many Santhals were forced to part with their land to the moneylenders or to the local landlords on usufructuary mortage.Since the loan could not be paid off, the land mortgaged could not be reclaimed.Most of the time a Santhal was forced to work as a wage labourer on his own land. The process of recovery in the land from the moneylender was also complex and expensive. It was this feeling of deprivation which led the Santhal to forcible harvesting of paddy in the late1960s. In fact, this was not a land grab movement but only a movement for reclaiming their lost land.

When the government introduced the concept of reserved and protected forest under its new policy of forest management, the rights of the Santhal in the forest were extinguished. The Santhal had a deep sense of identity with the forest and depend on it for their very existence. They believed that they were the lords of the forest and had an absolute right to use forest resources, both timber and non-timber, without the intervention of any external authority. The new forest policy, however, struck a blow to such thinking.The proclamation of protected and reserved forest within their traditional homeland led to the shrinkage of land available to the Santhal. The reclamation of land from the forest was their mechanism to meet the pressure of population growth. The small village forest left for their use was soon depleted and Santhals were forced to take up other sources of livelihood.

Earlier, the Santhal had great knowledge of the forest resources. Botillen (1996 : 141-147)[18] has given the names of leaves and plants used by the Santhal. With the disappearance of the forest, the wild fruits, mushrooms, gums, raisins and honey which they used to collect for food and for sale are not now available. Thus his dependence on nature has been greatly reduced.

Another component of the worldview is self-management (Roy Burman, 1992 : 35)[19]. It is tied up with systems of access to or control and the management of land and land-based resources. With the increasing loss of control over resources the notion of self-management is only confined to the socio-religious sphere. In recent times *disom sendra* (annual hunt) has become rare. This has confined the area of self-management largely to the village level. There also it is being threatened by the New Panchayati Raj which is to be introduced in the tribal areas. It is based on an entirely different electoral process. The traditional norms of Santhal democracy may have to be sacrificed to pave the way for uniformity.

Significant socio-economic changes are taking place in the world of the Santhal. New technologies in agriculture, irrigation, family planning and health, the concept of decentralization and people's participation are affecting the social order. The Santhal can no longer remain geographically or socially exclusive. The older generation is anxious to maintain the old social and moral order by invoking the great tradition emanating from the belief in the 'Santhal Raj'.The existing tradition of education, agriculture and health practices which is anchored in the old value system is facing new onslaughts. The Santhal is face-to-face with two worlds which are rooted in very different premises. This sometimes generates an attitude of ambivalence to its tradition and processes of modernization.

The idea of good life is integrally linked to the relationship between the social order and the moral order. Faced with challenges of the time, sometimes the propitiation of the supernatural order which determines the moral order also becomes intense and intimate. Martin Orans[20] who studied the Santhal around Jameshedpur has given many examples of such response.

The confrontation of technology and ritual is not a simplistic factor. A new technological system also tends to develop its own rituals but these call for less of intuition and more of reason. There has been a desperate attempt by the tribal elite to reinforce ethnic identity by devising an elaborate, historical, mythological account of tribal ancestry wih a golden shared past. There is stress on cultural exclusiveness and cultural revivalism. There is new emphasis on cultural forms, myths, symbols, scripts, oral literature, religious beliefs and traditional values. Some of these have been altered to fit in with the present ones, although the form and the name remain the same. In the early stages[21] of the Jharkhand Mukti Morcha Movement, great importance was given to the old Santhal institutions specially concerned with tribal self-government like the *Baisi* at different levels. In the same vein attempts were made at social reform particularly in banning the use of rice beer and liquor and regulating payment of *gonong* or bride price. A new script known as Ol Chiki was invented by Raghunath Murmu[22] so that the Santhals from Bihar , Bengal, Orissa could use a common script. The literature created by Raghunath Murmu is a reinterpretation of Santhali myth and tradition. Through his creative writing, plays and compilations, he has sought to socialize and culturize the entire concept of Santhal identity and solidarity. He has used myths, histories in his own idea to project a great tradition and called upon his tribe to live up to it. He tried to forge a sense of identity and create awareness.Thus the Santhal have tried to create, maintain and fight for the identity as well as their worldview in diverse ways through a selective borrowing of culture traits. They have been able to retain the essential features of their social and moral order without denying themselves the benefits of new development efforts.The worldview of the Santhal is characterized by both continuity and change. Their resilience is manifested in their values, attitudes and behaviour.

NOTES AND REFERENCES

1. Dube, S.C., 1988, *Modernization and Development : The Search for Alternative Paradigms.*

2. Badley, 1982, *Alternatives to Ethnocide in Western Expansions and Indigenous People.*

3. Archer, 1987, 'Remote Areas, Some Theoretical Contributions' in A.Jackson (Ed), *Anthropology of Home,* Tavistock Publications, London.

4. Sol Tax, 1941, World View and Social Relation in Guatemala, *American Anthropologist*, New Series, Vol 43.

5. Redfield, R., 1955, *The Primitive World and its Transformation* , Cornell University Press, Ithaca.

6. Geertz, C., 1968, 'Ethos, World View and Analysis of Sacred Symbols' in Alan Dundas (Ed) *Everyman His Way*, Prentice Hall, New Jersey.

7. Archer, W. G., 1974, *The Hill of Flutes : Life , Love and Poetry in Tribal India. A Portrait of the Santal,* George Allen & Unwin, London.

8. Quoted in, Archer, W.G. (1974)

9. Archer, W. G., 1974, *The Hills of Flutes.*

10. Troisi, J., 1978, *Tribal Religion : Religious Beliefs and Practices Among the Santal,* Manohar, Delhi.

11. *Statesman,* Calcutta, April 28,1978.

12. Evans-Pritchard, E.E., 1940, *The Nuer,* Oxford University Press, Oxford.

13. Mahapatra, S., 1983, 'Raghunath Murmu's movement for Santal Solidarity' in K.S.Singh (Ed) *Tribal Movements in India,* Vol II, Manohar, New Delhi.

14. Dutt, G.S., 1951, *Tribal Craftsmen in Census of West Bengal.*

15. Gautam, M.K., 1977, *In Search of an Identity : A Case of the Santhal of Northern India,* Leiden.

16. Datta-Majumdar, N., *The Santal : A study in Cultural Change,* A.S.I. Memoir No 2, Calcutta.

17. Mumford, L., *Technics and Civilization.*

18. Botillen, O., 1996, *Santals and Natural Resources of Jharkhand : An Ecological Anthropological Perspective,* Agricultural University of Norway, Oslo.

19. Roy Burman, B.K., 1992, 'Alternative World View' in Behura and Tripathi (Ed) *Science, Culture and Development,* Paragon Publishers, Bhubaneswar.

20. Orans, M., 1965, *The Santals : A tribe in Search of a Great Tradition,* Detroit.

21. Sachchidananda, 1991 (Special), The Santal Odyssey : A Quest for Identity, *Man in India.*

22. Mahapatra, S.K., 'Development and Culture' in Behura and Tripathi (Ed), *Science, Culture and Development,* Paragon Publishers, Bhubaneshwar.

# CONTRIBUTORS


| | |
|---|---|
| Ajit Kumar Aditya | Zoologist<br>Professor<br>Department of Zoology<br>Visva - Bharati<br>Santiniketan - 731235<br>West Bengal |
| Indrani Bhattacharyya (Chakraborty) | Anthropologist<br>20 C/E, Criper Road<br>P.O. Konnagar<br>Dist. Hooghly - 712235<br>West Bengal |
| Subhra Bhattacharyya | Anthropologist<br>Senior Research Fellow<br>Anthropological Survey of India<br>27, Jawaharlal Nehru Road<br>Calcutta - 700016<br>West Bengal |
| S. K. Chakraborty | Anthropologist<br>General Secretary<br>Raja Ram Mohan Roy Institute of Social and Development Anthropology<br>1 8/B Siddeswar Chandra Lane<br>Calcutta - 700012<br>West Bengal |
| Prasanta Chatterjee | Zoologist<br>Research Scholar<br>Department of Zoology<br>Visva - Bharati<br>Santiniketan - 731235<br>West Bengal |
| P.C. Hembram | Deputy Director General<br>Office of the Director General<br>All India Radio<br>Akashvani Bhavan<br>New Delhi - 110001 |

| | |
|---|---|
| Khageswar Mahapatra | Linguist<br>C-123, Housing Board Colony<br>Baramunda<br>Bhubaneshwar - 751003<br>Orissa |
| Sitakant Mahapatra | Anthropologist<br>21, Satyanagar<br>Bhubaneshwar - 751007 |
| Chaitanya Prasad Majhi | Columnist<br>Plot No. A/18<br>Unit VII, Suryanagar<br>Bhubaneshwar - 751003<br>Orissa |
| Nita Mathur | Anthropologist<br>Research Associate<br>Indira Gandhi National Centre for the Arts<br>Janpath<br>New Delhi - 110001 |
| Shyam Sundar Mohapatra | Folklorist<br>Professor<br>Department of Oriya<br>Visva - Bharati<br>Santiniketan - 731235<br>West Bengal |
| Peter Pannke | Musicologist<br>Egerstr. 12<br>14/93 Berlin<br>Germany |
| N. Patnaik | Anthropologist<br>Director<br>Social Science and Development Institute<br>Plot No. 1243<br>Nageswartangi, Lewis Road<br>Bhubaneshwar - 751002 |

| | |
|---|---|
| Onkar Prasad | Anthropologist<br>Professor<br>Palli Charcha Kendra<br>Visva - Bharati<br>Santiniketan - 731235<br>West Bengal |
| Nilanjana Das (Saha) | Artist<br>C/o Neoti Devnath<br>Shyambti, Canal Par<br>Santiniketan - 731235<br>West Bengal |
| Sachchidananda | Anthropologist<br>Director<br>Sulabh Institute Development Studies<br>Sulabh Bhavan, New Patliputra Colony<br>Patna - 800013<br>Bihar |
| Baidyanath Saraswati | Anthropologist<br>Unesco Professor<br>Indira Gandhi National Centre for the Arts<br>Janpath<br>New Delhi - 110001 |

# INDEX